Sociolinguistics: A Very Short Introduction

VERY SHORT INTRODUCTIONS are for anyone wanting a stimulating and accessible way in to a new subject. They are written by experts and have been published in more than 25 languages worldwide.

The series began in 1995 and now represents a wide variety of topics in history, philosophy, religion, science, and the humanities. The VSI library now contains more than 300 volumes—a Very Short Introduction to everything from ancient Egypt and Indian philosophy to conceptual art and cosmology—and will continue to grow in a variety of disciplines.

Very Short Introductions available now:

For more information visit our web site

www.oup.co.uk/general/vsi/

John Edwards

SOCIOLINGUISTICS

A Very Short Introduction

OXFORD
UNIVERSITY PRESS

OXFORD
UNIVERSITY PRESS

Oxford University Press is a department of the University of Oxford.
It furthers the University's objective of excellence in research,
scholarship, and education by publishing worldwide.

Oxford   New York

Auckland   Cape Town   Dar es Salaam   Hong Kong   Karachi
Kuala Lumpur   Madrid   Melbourne   Mexico City   Nairobi
New Delhi   Shanghai   Taipei   Toronto

With offices in

Argentina   Austria   Brazil   Chile   Czech Republic   France   Greece
Guatemala   Hungary   Italy   Japan   Poland   Portugal   Singapore
South Korea   Switzerland   Thailand   Turkey   Ukraine   Vietnam

Oxford is a registered trademark of Oxford University Press
in the UK and certain other countries.

Published in the United States of America by
Oxford University Press
198 Madison Avenue, New York, NY 10016

Library of Congress Cataloging-in-Publication Data
has been applied for

978-0-19-985861-3

7 9 8

Printed in Great Britain
by Ashford Colour Press Ltd., Gosport, Hants.
on acid-free paper

Do Dorren agus d'Oisín Ó Siochrú,
beirt a bhfuil grá mór agus
cion agam dóibh

Contents

Contents

List of illustrations

Acknowledgments

While I have drawn on the work of many colleagues here, direct help was provided by Paulin Djité, Tadhg Ó hIfearnáin, Geneva Smitherman, and Robert Zecker.

Chapter 1
Coming to terms

The acquisition of language cannot be accounted for solely on the basis of postnatal experience. Human beings must be genetically prepared or "pre-wired" to learn language. Since it would be silly to think that children born in France have a different sort of evolutionary wiring than their counterparts in Finland, brains must be equally "ready" in all the many language communities of the world. This, in turn, implies that at some fundamental level all languages may be cut from the same cloth. Noam Chomsky has been the single most important champion of this approach, in which linguistics intertwines with philosophy, psychology, and epistemology. All languages are not, of course, similar at more immediately observable levels, which means that linguists also concern themselves with the structure of words (morphology) or phrases (syntax), with meaning (semantics), with sound (phonology), and with lexicon (vocabulary). In effect, their work amounts to a detailed fleshing-out of the environmental "shaping" that directs the general genetic preparedness into specific language channels.

The environmental contexts of language are its obvious and immediate facets, and what might be called the "social life of language" has always been of great interest to a wide variety of people. Central here is the relationship between language and identity, whose consequences are always interesting and sometimes dramatic. A thousand years before the dawn of the modern era, some Ephraimites attempted to "pass" as Gileadites: they had been defeated and hoped to return home across the Jordan. They were detected, however, because of their inability when challenged to pronounce the word *shibboleth* in the Gileadite manner. In Judges 12:6, when the impostor "could not frame to pronounce it right . . . they took him, and slew him at the passages of Jordan" (KJV). More generally, and more peacefully, Publilius Syrus—once a slave, then a famous Roman epigrammatist—observed that "speech is a mirror of the soul." In the seventeenth century, John Locke wrote that language is the "great instrument and common tie" of society. And, in the twentieth, the linguist Edward Sapir argued that language was simply the most basic linchpin of humanity. In both its ordinary communicative role and as the most immediate symbolic marker of human affiliation, language is preeminently a social phenomenon.

Scholarly inquiry into sociolinguistics and the sociology of language can be traced to the nineteenth century, and no doubt existed much earlier. The terms used today, though, are relatively recent. Japanese scholars in the 1930s had proposed the uniting of sociology and linguistics, and the word *sociolinguistics* was apparently introduced by a Cambridge anthropologist, Thomas Hodson, in 1939. The single most important antecedent to modern study, however, appeared in 1952.

In that year, an assistant professor of English in Houston cited H. L. Mencken's *The American Language*, suggesting that its great popularity did not indicate a broad public concern with language or linguistics per se but, rather, that it was "socially satisfying or harrassing" to many people. Haver Currie was able to point to some existing American academic attention to those social aspects of language that interested Mencken's readers, but he lamented that the United States lagged behind Europe in the study of "folk" or "common" speech. Unaware of Hodson's coinage, Currie then suggested that a scholarly field called socio-linguistics [*sic*] might usefully be dedicated to the interaction of language and society.

2

Currie mentioned social status as a particularly interesting variable, foreshadowing a great amount of work in areas ranging from minority-majority group relations, to the ways in which different dialects are perceived, to the language of kinship terms and politeness. If, for example, languages and dialects can have greater or lesser prestige according to the standing of their speakers, it is equally clear that individuals may be given different titles (Dr., Mr., Ms.) and can be addressed at different levels of formality (John, Professor Smith). Formality is reflected in different personal pronouns: thus, *tu* or *vous* in French; *du* or *Sie* in German; *tú* or *usted* in Spanish. English has lost its earlier *thou–you* distinction, but it does retain the "royal *we*," the plural form used of an individual, historically related to power, and often the basis of the "respectful" variant of the second-person pronoun.

The sociology and the social psychology of language are, like sociolinguistics, concerned with the intertwining of language and society. Some have suggested that while the main focus of sociolinguistics is on language variation in different social contexts, the other terms imply an emphasis on behavior and context from a linguistic perspective. Others have argued that sociolinguistics is essentially the study of speakers' language choices; if so, a reciprocity of influence becomes immediately apparent. Context clearly affects such choices: we make different selections from our repertoire when talking to spouses, children, pets, vicars, doctors, friends in the bar, and so on. At the same time, however, language variation can be an important indicator of speakers' perceptions of particular settings and so may even act to alter their psychosocial tenor. A further distinction has seen sociolinguistics more interested in matters at a micro level than at a broader macro one.

Not only are terms and distinctions here treated quite loosely (sometimes within the same inquiry), there are other more specific headings under which the language-and-society nexus is studied. Included are applied linguistics, educational linguistics, anthropological linguistics, geolinguistics, and ethnolinguistics. These more fine-grained headings and perspectives are employed according to context and, often, to intent. It is probably not very fruitful to attempt further delineations along these lines, probably best to simply recognize that beyond the scope of linguistics per se, there is a related but often fairly independent set of approaches that consider society and language together.

Four final notes. First, although this is not a study of historical sociolinguistics, readers will note frequent historical allusions and examples. They are here to remind us that long before the modern terms now in familiar use, people were always deeply concerned about the social life of language. Second, when discussing languages and language groups, I have not put words like *small*, *big*, and *large* in the quotation marks that they really require. The terms denote the relative scope and dominance of languages, not the actual size of speech communities. More importantly, no value judgment is implied. Third, *multilingualism* could often replace *bilingualism* here (in considering fluency across different dimensions, for instance); the use of the latter term alone is simply in the interests of brevity and nonrepetition. Fourth, representation of letters and pronunciations departs from technical convention—this, simply in the service of greater reader-friendliness.

Language, dialect, and accent

It has become fashionable in some academic quarters to deny that languages actually exist, at least as "separable and enumerable categories." Languages are social constructions or inventions that vary across both communities and individuals. There are overlaps, sharp boundaries are generally lacking, and repertoires are dynamic and not unchanging. Indeed, at the level of the *idiolect*—the language of the individual—no two of us are exactly alike. Nonetheless, for all ordinary intents and purposes, there *are* separate languages, and there *are* distinct varieties within them.

There are interesting debates about nonhuman systems of communication. Is it right to speak of the "language" of some primates, of bees, porpoises, and whales, or should the label only be applied to human beings? Whatever the preferred answer, no one would deny that human language is far and away the most complex of all mediums. It does not, as other nonhuman systems do, merely reflect instinctual and largely invariant responses to immediate stimuli. On the contrary, we can discuss events in both the past and the future, we can contemplate things that never existed and never will. This nuance is possible because all members of a language community agree, first of all, on the meanings of things that reflect, in themselves, arbitrary choices. There is nothing intrinsic in either the sound "table," or its representation on the page, that conjures up the familiar meaning. It "works" in English but not in German or Japanese, where the community has come to assign different sounds and symbols to that same concept.

Second, we collectively agree upon certain rules—the grammar of a language—which are, again, entirely arbitrary. With a set of elements (words or components of words) and a system that regulates their combinations, there emerges a language capable of more or less infinite creativity. With a little thought, it would be possible for almost all of us to come up with a sentence that has probably never been uttered or written before; a reasonable knowledge of elements-plus-rules should permit the deciphering of its meaning. This knowledge also allows us to separate sentences that are nonsensical but grammatical ("Colorless green ideas sleep furiously") from those that are both nonsensical and ungrammatical ("Furiously sleep ideas green colorless"). Note, too, that what "works" as nonsensical-but-grammatical in one language will not do so in another. "'Twas brillig and the slithy toves" is *English* nonsense, and *Jabberwocky* would have to be dramatically recast—as has been done—to turn it into either *Das Jammerwoch* or *Le Jaseroque*.

1. Sir John Tenniel drew this illustration for Lewis Carroll's *Through the Looking-Glass, and What Alice Found There* (1871). It shows the monster described in Carroll's famous nonsense poem *Jabberwocky*.

All of this suggests a powerful but delicate human language capacity. For a long time, observers as varied as Ludwig Wittgenstein (philosopher), Otto Jespersen (linguist), and Charles-Maurice de Talleyrand (politician) have pointed out that the central characteristic of language is the capacity for storytelling, for hiding rather than revealing, for fiction and falsehood.

Most languages have a number of relatives, sharing some common familial features. However, even speakers of closely related varieties—Spanish and Italian, for instance—cannot expect full mutual comprehension, and reciprocal unintelligibility clearly increases with linguistic distance. Indeed, one would expect no overlapping between Finnish and Haida. As subvarieties under a common language roof, *dialects* are formally defined as mutually intelligible variants, differing one from another along three dimensions: vocabulary, grammar, and pronunciation. In some English dialects, speakers *brew* their tea; others let it *mash*, or *sit*, or *steep*. In others, *frying-pans* become *skillets*, and *milk shakes* become *frappes* or perhaps even *cabinets*. Few would deny that these lexical variants are anything other than different from one another or would assert that *bonnet* is better than *hood*, that *boot* makes more sense than *trunk*, that *tube* is more appropriate than *subway*. (Simple translation between British and American variants does not exhaust the complexity, of course. Like the Americans, the British have trunks, but not on their cars; their cars have hoods, which are not their bonnets; and Americans without cars can travel on the subway, something that the English can only walk through.)

When it comes to grammatical variation, however, many people are rather less tolerant: when, for instance, they hear someone say, "I done it yesterday," or "I ain't never goin' there again," or "I ax Billy can he play tomorrow." There is in fact ample scholarly evidence that *all* dialects are valid systems of communication, and that none is intrinsically better or worse than another. It is logical to assume that every group of speakers has a communication system that works for them with the precision called for in their social circumstances and without ambiguity. It is illogical to think that some groups manage to get by without such a system. Speakers of all dialects, then, speak correctly. The only appropriate yardsticks of correctness are community norms. Problems arise because not all communities and dialects have equal social clout, because the linguistic standards of those in power become dominant, and because social dominance (in language as elsewhere) allows difference to be translated into deficiency.

A final word here about dialects and their presumed mutual intelligibility. The inhabitants of Tangier Island in Chesapeake Bay certainly speak English, but their dialect is virtually impenetrable for mainland American speakers. On the other side of the ocean, a popular English television program, *Auf Wiedersehen, Pet*, depicted the adventures of a gang of unemployed bricklayers, one or two of whom had such thick Geordie varieties—the working-class dialect of Newcastle-upon-Tyne—that letters in the newspaper from viewers in the south of England requested subtitles. Indeed, most of us have encountered varieties of our own language that fail the mutual-intelligibility test.

Robert Burns famously wrote in Scots—also known as "braid [broad] Scots," or "Lallans [Lowlands] Scots"; here is a verse from his familiar *Auld Lang Syne*, written in 1788 and sung around the world on New Year's Eve (or Hogmanay, in Scots):

> We twa hae run about the braes;
> And pu'd the gowans fine;
> But we've wander'd mony a weary fit,
> Sin' auld lang syne.

A couple of centuries after Burns, I visited Edinburgh and went to Suruchi—an Indian restaurant—where the menu opened with these words:

8

We're gaunae wheech ye aff for a whilie—aff tae yer ain pairt o India, whaur ye'll eat thae dishes that maist fowk in India eats. Tho Britain is hoatchin wi "curry shops" the day, in Scotland we're skiffin the surface yet . . .

Among the food on offer: *popadoms* (plain yins or spicy yins); *murgh sagwala* (tender dauds o chucken cookit wi reamed spinach, ingans, green herbs an guid reekin spices); and *chucken tikka masala* (the hail jing bang o fowk in Britain loo this dish an noo it's cookit tae the Suruchi's unique receipt). Readers may reasonably ask if guid braid Scots is an English dialect or a separate language.

Finally, suppose that there are four dialect communities, A, B, C, and D. Suppose that speakers of A and B can easily understand one another, that those in groups A and C have some considerable difficulty, and that speakers of A and D simply cannot communicate. Does this mean that A and D are actually different languages? Those unaware of groups B and C might be forgiven for thinking so, but they might not if the full continuum were revealed to them. The suggestion made by the linguist and Yiddishist Max Weinreich that "a language is a dialect that has an army and navy" illustrates another point of confusion between languages and dialects. Speakers of Norwegian and Danish can understand each other well—Swedish might go into the mix, as well—but the demands of political identity require that their varieties are styled languages. A similar situation applies to Hindi and Urdu, to Czech and Slovak, and to other pairs and triplets.

The story of Serbo-Croatian is a rather poignant example of social interference in the name of identity. The language was a common variety among not just Serbs and Croats but also Bosnians and Montenegrins. There were, to be sure, internal variants, pressures, and complaints, but the language as such was widely used and accepted. With the breakup of Yugoslavia, Serbo-Croatian lost its official existence, to be replaced by Bosnian, Serbian, and Croatian.

In Serbia little has actually happened; indeed, one of those earlier complaints was that the language was too "Serbianized" a medium anyway. In Bosnia, moves to emphasize Arabic-Turkish features have been made, but basic grammar and lexicon have been little affected. In Croatia, though, a number of symbolic declarations have been accompanied by formal efforts to try and make two languages where one once existed. Scholars are thus employed to set up barriers to communication in the cause of an exclusionary group solidarity.

Within dialect, there are also important variants and perceptions at the level of accent or pronunciation, and some other within-language distinctions—such as style, register, slang, and jargon—will be touched upon later in the book.

Instrument and symbol

The communicative function of languages and their subvarieties does not exhaust their importance. Languages are also potent boundary markers, highlighting and labeling particular social memberships: they are symbols of group identity. This is not something people think about very much, perhaps, if they belong to a community whose language is one of the current "languages of wider communication" like English, Spanish, Chinese, and Arabic. For speakers of these varieties the communicative and the symbolic aspects coincide, and the language of daily life is also that in which the group's traditions, history, and literature are recorded. Those whose mother tongue is a smaller language, however, often find their original or ancestral language becoming more and more a symbolic medium. Symbolic aspects of life can still figure importantly in self-perception; in fact, their very lack of tangible or visible substance can give them strength and staying power. Still, although psychologically important language status can long remain after the partial or full eclipse of mundane instrumentality, symbolic status arises from ordinary vernacular use—not the reverse. A shift away from a language in its ordinary communicative role must lead eventually to the dilution and ultimate disappearance of its symbolic significance.

Language families

How did human language arise? Was there *one* original variety (the principle of *monogenesis*) or did several emerge more or less simultaneously, in different places (*polygenesis*)? Putting these questions together with what is known about the world's five thousand languages, considering that these are collected in as many as two or three hundred language families, and realizing that these families are components in still larger groupings, makes the idea of some original linguistic tree trunk(s) seem logical, if only theoretically supportable. Hard data evaporate over time, and even contemporary relationships are not always clear. Where some scholars would perceive a separate family, others would see a thick branch of an existing group, and this accounts for the widely varying estimates of language-family numbers.

Some might think that reference to language classifications and families is of narrow linguistic interest and not a great concern for more "social" attention. This is wrong on both general and specific counts. The ever-increasing knowledge about such groupings relies upon scholarly triangulation, in which evidence from language patterns and similarities is combined with archaeological, historical, and genetic information to produce an informative *social* picture of past and present communities. More specifically, chapter 8 shows how languages, and the possible relationships among them, have historically loomed large in some of the deepest religious questions.

Speculation about families of languages had been abroad for more than a century when Sir William ("Oriental") Jones gave the idea its "academic identity card" in a 1784 address to the Asiatick Society of Bengal, suggesting strong affinities among Sanskrit, Greek, and Latin. One of his biographers has called

Jones the "father of modern linguistics" and, while this may be overly generous, he was clearly one of the first scholars of comparative and historical linguistics. His description of Latin and Greek as "sisters" having a common "parent" marked the beginning of serious attention to what would soon be called the "Indo-European" languages and, more widely, to cross-language comparisons that went beyond varieties in geographical proximity. The work took some time to gear up, however, and the nineteenth-century studies of Jacob Grimm, Franz Bopp, Rasmus Rask, and other continental scholars provided the first firm bases. A historical approach to language classification was distinctly appealing in Darwin's century; so, as with earlier linguistic analogues to herbals and bestiaries, language families came to be understood as products and reflections of evolutionary development. Beyond the Indo-European group of languages, other important assemblies include the Austronesian, Niger-Congo, Afro-Asiatic, and Sino-Tibetan families. The greatest number of speakers (about 2.5 billion) is found among the 450 Indo-European languages, but the Niger-Congo and Austronesian families, each with about 350 million speakers, reveal much greater language diversity: there are more than 1,500 languages in the former, and almost 1,300 in the latter.

Box A
Sir William Jones on Sanskrit, 1784

The *Sanscrit* language, whatever be its antiquity, is of a wonderful structure; more perfect than the *Greek*; more copious than the *Latin*, and more exquisitely refined than either, yet bearing to both of them a stronger affinity, both in the roots of verbs and in the forms of grammar, than could possibly have been produced by accident; so strong indeed, that no philologer could examine them all three, without believing them to have sprung from some common source, which, perhaps, no longer exists.

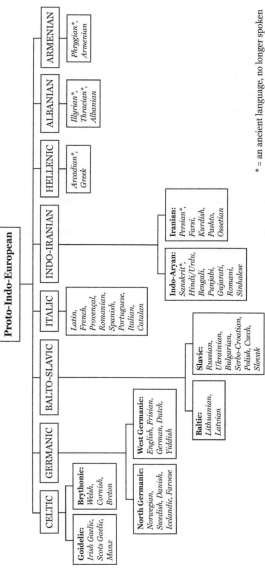

The Indo-European Family Tree: An Abridged Depiction

Proto-Indo-European

CELTIC

- **Goidelic:** *Irish Gaelic, Scots Gaelic, Manx*
- **Brythonic:** *Welsh, Cornish, Breton*

GERMANIC

- **North Germanic:** *Norwegian, Swedish, Danish, Icelandic, Faroese*
- **West Germanic:** *English, Frisian, German, Dutch, Yiddish*

BALTO-SLAVIC

- **Baltic:** *Lithuanian, Latvian*
- **Slavic:** *Russian, Ukrainian, Bulgarian, Serbo-Croatian, Polish, Czech, Slovak*

ITALIC

Latin, French, Provençal, Romanian, Spanish, Portuguese, Italian, Catalan

INDO-IRANIAN

- **Indo-Aryan:** *Sanskrit*, Hindi/Urdu, Bengali, Punjabi, Gujarati, Romani, Sinhalese*
- **Iranian:** *Persian*, Farsi, Kurdish, Pashto, Ossetian*

HELLENIC

Arcadian*, Greek

ALBANIAN

Illyrian*, Thracian*, Albanian

ARMENIAN

Phrygian*, Armenian

* = an ancient language, no longer spoken

2. The Indo-European family tree has many branches. Only some of the more central ones are shown here—but enough to reveal the great diversity among the languages of the group.

13

Some languages, known as "isolates," have resisted family classification. This is (unsurprisingly) true for varieties known only because of classical references: ancient Cappadocian, for example, or Bithynian and Pontic. But modern Basque is also an isolate, thought to be a relic of pre–Indo-European Europe. Ainu, the language of a group in Japan who are physically unlike the Japanese themselves, is another example, as are the languages of the Salish and Kootenay peoples of British Columbia. So, too, is the now-extinct language of the Beothuks in Newfoundland. This society was ruthlessly slaughtered by Europeans—sometimes with the assistance of Indian mercenaries from the mainland—and the last speaker died of disease in St. John's in 1829. It is ironic that this people should have been the one to prompt the generic term "Red Indian": when John Cabot (Giovanni Caboto) first encountered the Beothuks in the late fifteenth century, he observed and reported their custom of rubbing themselves with red ochre.

Chapter 2
Variation and change

Variation is the only linguistic constant. Since, at base, sociolinguistics is about the linkages between language and society, inquiries into language variation are central: they lead to finer-grained understanding of these linkages by illuminating the changes that all natural languages are heir to. English speakers once sounded the "k" and the "g" in words like *knave*, *knight*, and *gnaw* and the "w" and "b" in *sword* and *lamb*. Why did they stop? Where change implies the possibility of impaired or imperfect communication, why does it occur? Historical and contemporary insight into languages and cultures in contact can answer these questions, revealing that change happens in non-random ways.

Besides pronunciation, grammar and vocabulary also alter over time, and their combined evolution can make our own language foreign to us. *Beowulf*, written about 1000 CE in the West Saxon dialect, is the classic poem of Old English literature. The opening sentence is:

Hwæt. We Gardena in geardagum,
þeodcyninga, þrym gefrunon,
hu ða æþelingas ellen fremedon.

Here are two modern translations: the first is by Michael Alexander (1973), the second by Seamus Heaney (2000):

> Attend!
> We have heard of the thriving of the throne of Denmark,
> how the folk-kings flourished in former days,
> how those royal athelings earned that glory.
>
> So. The Spear-Danes in days gone by
> and the kings who ruled them had courage and greatness.
> We have heard of those princes' heroic campaigns.

Apart from the obvious difficulty the original poses for modern English speakers, the passage also highlights orthographical change. We see the old letters *thorn* "þ" and *eth* "ð," each sounding more or less like "th," as well as the linkage (formally a "ligature") that produces "æ." The letters are gone in modern English, and the ligature is increasingly rare. All three continue to exist, however, in other alphabets—notably modern Icelandic. The two modern renditions suggest the inadequacy of any simple word-for-word approach; they also reveal the variation possible in translations of the same text.

Moving from Old English (ca. 450–1100 CE) to the period of Middle English (ca. 1100–1500), one finds a famous little round song; written ca. 1250, it is one of the earliest pieces that can be reasonably easily read today. (The old "long s"—the "ſ"—as well as the *thorn*, are shown in the original here.) This is the first verse:

> Svmer is icumen in,
> Lhude ſing cuccu.
> Groweþ ſed and bloweþ med
> And ſpringþ þe wde ["wode" or "wude"] nu
> Sing cuccu.

This becomes, in a contemporary rendering:

> Summer is here.
> Sing loudly, cuckoo.

The seed is sprouting and the meadows are blooming,
And the woods spring into life.
Sing, cuckoo!

Chaucer's *Canterbury Tales* (ca. 1390) is still in the Middle English period. The prologue begins:

Whan that aprill with his shoures soote
The droghte of march hath perced to the roote,
And bathed every veyne in swich licour
Of which vertu engendred is the flour;

Again, modern readers will be able to grasp most of this, although "bilingual" editions of Chaucer are still quite usual.

The works of Shakespeare and Dickens provide examples of Early Modern English (1500–1750) and Modern English (from 1750), respectively. Here, first, are some lines spoken by Romeo, as they appeared in the first folio edition of *Romeo and Juliet* (act 1, scene 4):

A Torch for me, let wantons light of heart
Tickle the ſenceleſſe ruſhes with their heeles:
For I am prouerb'd with a Grandſier Phraſe,
Ile be a Candle-holder and looke on,
The game was nere ſo faire, and I am done.

(The "long s" is again retained here, as is the "u" for "v" in the third line.) With the possible exception of *grandsier* (i.e., grandfather, or ancestor), there are no words that cannot be understood here; still, many readers will need at least some assistance in decoding the passage today.

Finally, even the works of Dickens—those perennial favorites for modern television drama—pose some difficulties for the contemporary reader. Here are two passages taken from *David Copperfield* (published 1849–50):

The conflicting interests of these touting gentlemen being of a nature to irritate their feelings, personal collisions took place; and the Commons was even scandalised by our principal inveigler (who had formerly been in the wine trade, and afterwards in the sworn brokery line) . . .

In pursuance of my intention of referring to my own fictions only when their course should incidentally connect itself with the progress of my story, I do not enter on the aspirations, the delights, anxieties and triumphs of my art.

From *Beowulf* to Chaucer to Dickens: the progression of difficulty illustrated here is borne out by several years' worth of investigation with my university students, who are given some context and, of course, told about "þ" and "ð," and "ſ." By the time we get to Dickens, vocabulary problems have abated but stylistic hindrances remain. Increasingly rare in English classes at both secondary and university level, the works of Dickens may soon require the translations or annotations that accompany earlier works.

For tracking grammatical and lexical changes over time, there are written and printed texts (not always enough of them, of course). For past pronunciation changes, however, there are no direct data records, no speech samples. In the Great (English) Vowel Shift that gradually proceeded over the two centuries between Chaucer and Shakespeare, the long vowels moved: for example, *time* once sounded like *teem*, *house* like *hoose*, and *day* like *die*. Such non-random alterations often involve "chain shifts," by which sounds move along a phonetic spectrum: linguists write of "push" and "pull" chains, a sort of regularized game of musical chairs in which a sound move creates a vacancy into which an adjacent sound can move, and so on. A New Zealander delighting over the purchase of a lovely new *rid driss* is demonstrating part of a chain shift that has "raised" the vowel: just as *bad* has come to sound like *bed*, so *bed* must then move to sound like *bid*.

The investigation of historical changes in pronunciation requires some detective work. The relationships among languages offer clues: until that Middle English vowel shift, the English pronunciation of the letters *B, C,* and *D* was as it now remains in French (*bay, say, day*). Scholars also attend to the ways poets and dramatists of the past scanned their sentences and rhymed their words. Phonetic spellings and misspellings found in all sorts of written material are also useful. If words such as *marchants* and *parsons* regularly appear in print and if it is clear that the writers were referring to *merchants* and *persons*, that is a clue to pronunciation.

Modern studies in language variation

Given sufficient interest—for forensic purposes, for instance—it could be shown that no two people speak exactly alike. However small a dialect or accent group may be, and however fine-grained the restriction to specific styles or registers or jargons, at least some variation could still be found at the individual idiolectal level. Age and gender differences also make their presence felt, across individuals but still within the smallest of groups, and teasing these out may sometimes be desirable. Charting large-scale variation across time, however, is usually of greatest general interest, and contemporary linguists now have more tools to accomplish this. Most obvious and relevant is the use of sound (and video) recording with written transcription.

Thanks in part to the archived recordings of Queen Elizabeth's Christmas messages, for example, sociolinguists can demonstrate that she has changed her pronunciation throughout her sixty years on the throne. While it is unlikely that Her Majesty will ever drop her aitches, she no longer speaks her own original Queen's English. This variety, traditionally taken as the apex of "Received Pronunciation" (RP), has moved closer to a standard southern British English (see p. 24). Of course, the queen need not pay the slightest attention to changing usage in general or to her own speech in particular, and she could cite an old regal precedent. At the Council of Constance, convened in 1414 to discuss heresy, schism, and church reform, Emperor Sigismund's language was corrected by a minion. His lofty reply: *"ego sum rex romanus, et supra grammaticam"* (I am the king of Rome, and above grammar).

Sociolinguistic fieldwork can be direct—asking people to say things that have the linguistic features of interest or probing for vocabulary differences across regions—or it can be a bit more subtle. Investigators can listen, record, and re-listen as required. The value of written information, however, has not been entirely displaced. Some very recent work has compared interview and questionnaire methods, finding that the latter still have a place. They can produce reliable data in response to these sorts of questions: "Does 'news' sound like *nyooze* or *nooze*?" "Does 'leisure' rhyme with *measure*, or with *seizure*?" "What do you call the knob you turn to get water in a sink?"

The first published report of this type appeared more than a century ago, and it was a strikingly large undertaking. Rather than conducting field interviews, Georg Wenker sent questionnaires investigating phonetic and grammatical variation to village schools throughout Germany. The forms presented forty sentences for teachers to send back to him in the dialect of the area: that is, they had to make orthographical adaptations in an attempt to capture local pronunciation. Wenker apparently received some 52,000 questionnaires, so it is perhaps unsurprising that only very partial results appeared in his *Sprach-Atlas von Nord- und Mitteldeutschland*, published in 1881.

The single greatest disadvantage of this sort of approach is that it relies upon self-reported data. It may be problematic when asking how words rhyme—informants may not always be entirely honest. It is certainly problematic when interpretation must rely upon amateur phonetic and orthographic efforts. Realization of the difficulties is part of the rationale for "ethnographic" studies, in which close and sustained cultural investigations are carried out by scholars who try to become group insiders, and whose results thus emerge from "participant observation." This method has also led to the generation of more indirect measures.

One pioneer of modern variationist sociolinguistics is William Labov. In work reported in the early 1960s, he investigated language use on Martha's Vineyard, an island just off the Massachusetts coast whose population swells dramatically with tourists during the summer. In something like a return to the pronunciation of the first English settlers in Massachusetts, words like *light* began to sound more like *loight*. Labov found that the motivation for such alteration, which began with local fishermen, was social in nature: it represented a way of distinguishing themselves from the summer visitors, who were (as such visitors so often are) both welcomed and resented. The change was then adopted by others on the island, even though such "vocal centralization" is not a generally prestigious feature in either American or British English. Since it is clear that socially based change is also implicated in regional distinctiveness, geographical and social or class distinctiveness are best considered together. It is a sense of identity, as marked through language, that is at the heart of things.

The "socialness" that is so important is what led Labov to initially resist the label of "sociolinguistics" on the simple grounds that it was impossible to conceive of a thoroughgoing linguistics which was *not* social. "Either our theories are about the language that ordinary people use on the street, arguing with friends, or at home blaming their children," he wrote, "or they are about very little indeed."

"Ordinariness" is key here, since the interest is typically in speech, in various contexts, which is not self-conscious or aware of being attended to in any formal way. In some of his work, Labov tried to elicit unselfconscious usage by asking respondents to discuss emotional issues, including death and danger, sex, and perceived injustice. Involvement in such discussions does seem to trump self-attention, but the context is still not as "natural" as it could be, and elements of the "observer's paradox" may arise to confound results. Labov put the matter this way: "to obtain the data most important for linguistic theory, we have to observe how people speak when they are not being observed."

The Martha's Vineyard setting illustrates change from "below," a more or less unconscious alteration. Later work on vowel shifts also shows change welling up from below. Speaking in an interview in 1991, Labov observed that important changes had been under way in American English for about half a century: in the interview, Labov himself illustrates the *sight* to *soight* sort of change noted earlier. Indeed, vowel alterations are underway around the Great Lakes, in the South, in California, and elsewhere. (In further testament to the language dynamism recorded by Labov, researchers who revisited Martha's Vineyard forty years after his work there found that the changes he described were evaporating, as closer and less traditional links to the mainland developed.)

In work that has become famous for its clever simplicity, for the way in which it elicited information without alerting the informants but also without crossing any ethical boundaries, Labov went on to illustrate change from "above." Here the topic is the use (or not) of the "postvocalic r." Speakers who exhibit "rhoticity" pronounce the "r" when it follows a vowel (as in *cart* or *flower*), while "non-rhotic" speakers do not—although they too sound the "r" when there is a following vowel (either in one word, as in *horrid* or in a sequence such as *flower opening*). Staff members in New York shops at the top, middle, and lower end of the market (Saks, Macy's, and Klein's, respectively) were asked by Labov (who is "rhotic") where specific goods were to be found. In every case, it had been predetermined that the items in question were on the "fourth floor." Since the respondents typically replied to the question twice—initially in a casual fashion and then, prompted by the questioner who apparently didn't quite catch their answer, more emphatically—there were at least four opportunities for Labov to hear whether the postvocalic "r" was pronounced. It was most frequently present in Saks, less frequent in Macy's, and least frequent of all in Klein's. Since rhoticity is a feature of more prestigious accents in New York English, the suggestion is that the staff members in higher-status shops were adopting the pronunciation of their customers. In this and related studies, Labov was able to show that patterns of pronunciation (and syntax) were regularly correlated with socioeconomic status. Later work by others has confirmed the continuation of such patterns.

Social tendencies and attitudes and, therefore, language variations are not always stable over time. They need not cross geographical boundaries, either. To stay with the letter "r" for a moment, there is a striking example of how regular convention in one setting may be quite different in another. While the use of the postvocalic "r" increases as one ascends the social ladder in New York, it is quite otherwise elsewhere. Nearly a decade after the famous department store studies, Peter Trudgill found a neatly inverted set of results in Reading, England.

Box B
Percentages of postvocalic "r" pronunciation in New York and Reading

	New York	Reading
Upper-middle-class speakers	32%	0%
Lower-middle-class speakers	20%	28%
Upper-working-class speakers	12%	44%
Lower-working-class speakers	10%	49%

It is not only English speakers in Berkshire who show this "un-American" pattern; non-rhoticity is a central feature of "Received Pronunciation" (RP: the prestigious and nonregional variety of British English; "received" is in the sense of "accepted as correct"). Equally, the New York results apply far beyond the city limits. At the same time, one need not go very far from New York to find American complexities: upper-crust Bostonians may not be non-rhotic in quite the same way as speakers of RP, but they often "pahk the cah" without an "r." The power of social convention regarding rhoticity is further demonstrated by the fact that most if not all English variants were once rhotic. It is only from the early seventeenth century that a gradual loss of the postvocalic "r" in some dialects can be observed. The reasons for accent change may not be clear, but it is safe to assume that, as with dialect variants, pronunciation difference typically becomes yet another aspect of status-boundary marking. This has nothing to do with any intrinsic correctness, virtue, or superiority, and everything to do with social pressure and prestige.

Considering that sound variations, to say nothing of lexical and grammatical regionalisms, have been shown to impede comprehension across cities and regions, and to interfere with cross-age-group communication within them, it is clear that powerful forces are at work. If unchecked and given sufficient time, these forces could drive in such strong linguistic wedges that dialect variations would enlarge to the point that separate languages could eventually emerge. The evolution of Latin into the various Romance languages is the classic case here. One might also bear in mind the rise around the world of a number of different Englishes, many of them well entrenched, with millions of speakers, and fast developing wide ranges of localisms. Might Indian English one day become entirely unintelligible to a speaker from Bristol, or Boston, or Brisbane? As Labov noted himself, there *are* countervailing pressures that militate against such an eventual mutual unintelligibility; chief among these are physical and social mobility of all sorts, as well as the ubiquity of print and the broadcast media. Whether these will prove in all cases to be sufficiently strong is not entirely clear, though.

Change may also rest to some (slight) degree upon desirable simplifications, and long-standing pronunciation differences may eventually be reflected in written language. It is easier to say *hambag* than *handbag*, and pronouncing it "properly" might seem pedantic or affected. It is also easier to leave off final consonants: many pronounce words like *running* and *jumping* without the final "g." Even such a simple and familiar example can reveal temporal, class, and gender dimensions. For instance, *huntin'*, *shootin'*, and *fishin'* were pronunciations once commonly used by the squire and the lord of the manor. They were also prone to drop the "h" with words like *hotel* and *historian*. While such usages were sometimes fashionable affectations, they exemplify an interesting complication: they were found at the two ends of the social-class scale. In the same way, *feller* (for *fellow*) and *ain't*, while continuingly frequent lower-class variants, were once also heard among the gentry but virtually never among the middle classes.

John Fischer's 1958 study was a reminder that gender is also a relevant factor here. Working with two dozen young children in New England, he investigated the use of the *in'* and *ing* endings (in words like *coming* and *going*). He found that boys were more likely than girls to use the former, and that the use of the latter increased with the formality of the situation. To this finding can be added a wealth of informal but accurate observation along contemporary social-class lines, but Fischer demonstrated that an awareness of the demands of more "polite" settings was in place, and that girls were more sensitive to this than were the boys, even among children younger than ten. (It has been suggested, incidentally, that the dropped "g" reflects an original pronunciation and the "educated" variant is a more modern introduction. Perhaps, then, it was nineteenth-century hypercorrection that produced the sounded "g.")

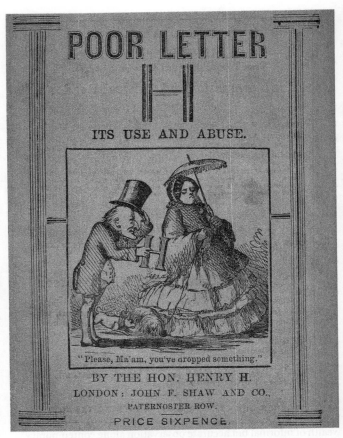

POOR LETTER

H

ITS USE AND ABUSE.

"Please, Ma'am, you've dropped something."

BY THE HON. HENRY H.
LONDON: JOHN F. SHAW AND CO.,
PATERNOSTER ROW.
PRICE SIXPENCE.

3. Some 50,000 copies of this short pamphlet, *Poor Letter H: Its Use and Abuse* (1854), had been sold by the 1860s. Its popularity reflects the increasing nineteenth-century attention to "correct" usage.

Although in British English words (like *house*) the "h" clearly had to be pronounced by anyone of social standing, it had been considered acceptable to drop it with words of Latin-French origin (*humour*, *hospital*, and so on). Attitudes gradually altered, however, and by the end of the nineteenth century only *heir*, *honour*, *honest*, and *hour* remained "h-less" in polite parlance. The "h" in words like *hotel* and *human* was now pronounced. Writing in 1873, Thomas Kington-Oliphant referred to "h" as "the fatal letter": dropping it was a "hideous barbarism." A century later, the phonetician John Wells wrote that dropping one's aitches had become "the single most powerful pronunciation shibboleth in England"—a "ready marker of social difference, a symbol of the social divide," as Lynda Mugglestone added. In *My Fair Lady*, Eliza Doolittle described the weather in three English counties: "in 'artford, 'ereford and 'ampshire, 'urricanes 'ardly hever 'appen" ('artford = Hertford, generally pronounced as "Hartford"). Indeed, Cockneys and others on the wrong side of the divide persist in omitting the "h" where it "ought" to appear, and sometimes inserting it where it shouldn't ("bring the heggs into the 'ouse, would you?"). Attempting to remedy these "errors," speakers may occasionally make embarrassing hypercorrections: pronouncing *heir* as if it were *hair* or *hare*, for example.

While the term "hypercorrection" can refer to *any* linguistic attempt to move up the social ladder, it most typically occurs where speakers of nonstandard dialects—feeling uneasy about socially nonprestigious features of their speech—tend to use higher-status variants, especially in formal settings. Labov found that in some very formal settings, lower-class speakers' use of such variants actually surpassed that of his upper-middle-class informants. Further, when asked about their customary linguistic practices, the former tended to exaggerate their use of higher-status forms. In many instances, hypercorrection involves the misapplication of rules, or overgeneralization. If, for instance, someone says "coupon" as *kyōō'pon* instead of *kōō'pon*, it likely stems from the mistaken belief that, if higher-status speakers say *styōōd'nt* rather than *stōōd'nt*, then an analogous pronunciation must be "correct" for *coupon*.

If nonstandard speakers sometimes imitate more standard ones, the opposite can also be true: features of working-class speech may be used by middle-class males, particularly when they wish to appear forceful, direct, and unambiguous; they may also claim greater use of these features than is actually the case. This "covert prestige" rests upon perceptions of what seems vibrant, masculine, and "tough," of what has "street cred." An illustrative example involved a middle-aged, upper-middle-class American university professor. He was being pressed by two or three male colleagues on an academic matter and, after an inconclusive discussion conducted in the educated dialect appropriate to the region, he finally stopped short, smiled broadly, and said, "Look fellas, you know they ain't no way I can do it!" This was a signal, immediately understood by all, that the time had come to cut to the chase. Conversation over. All-male social gatherings often produce such examples. The essence here lies in the perceived contrast between direct and no-nonsense usage, on the one hand, and inflated, tendentious, or blatantly dishonest language, on the other: straight shooting versus humbug (or "bullshit," now itself the object of increased scholarly scrutiny—and under that very name).

Covert prestige is essentially a male phenomenon—and, indeed, women may sometimes claim more *standard* usage than actually employed. The masculinity of nonstandard usage that underpins the operation of covert prestige is in some sense the mirror image of the alleged "poshness" or effeminacy associated with "talking proper" or, indeed, with generally educated usage. Orwell once observed that "nearly every Englishman of working-class origin considers it effeminate to pronounce foreign words correctly," and recent research suggests that the tendency continues.

Language change also occurs through outright borrowing: contemporary vernacular Japanese, for instance, has incorporated several thousand English "loan" words—loans that are rarely repaid. There are several varieties of this linguistic transfer. In the Japanese context it is common for English words to be sounded (and in some cases written) in ways that make them more immediately assimilable: *aisu kurimu* (ice cream), or *apato* (apartment), or *koin randori* (coin laundry). These are only somewhat stronger instances of the common practice of giving foreign borrowings a native-like pronunciation: to pronounce *pullover* in French as "poolovaire," or to make the French *garage* sound like "garridge" in English. In other types of transfer, however, original (or near-original) pronunciations are retained: for example, most English uses of terms like *raison d'être* or *savoir faire*, or, in anglophone Québec, the adoption of *dépanneur* (corner shop). Social-class marking can often be observed here, too: recall Orwell's observation about resistance to foreign pronunciation, on the one hand, and think of wine-and-food snobs on the other. (There are also "within-language" snobs. Hyacinth Bucket, in the popular BBC series *Keeping up Appearances*, insisted that her surname was pronounced *Bouquet*.)

A less well-known form of borrowing involves translations of loan words, such that *calques* (lit., "copies") are produced: the English "skyscraper" becomes *wolkenkratzer* (lit., cloud scraper) in German or *gratte-ciel* (lit., sky scraper) in French; the French *marché aux puces* is taken into English as "flea market." And finally, there are cross-language borrowings that are no longer recognized as such: *alcohol* and *algebra* have come into English from Arabic; *gazette* was originally the name of a Venetian coin; *punch* derives from a Sanskrit word via Hindi meaning "five" (because the traditional drink recipe called for five ingredients: alcohol, water or milk, sugar, spice, and lemon).

A more personal sort of borrowing is conversational "code-switching," a phenomenon that can occur within or across languages. Variations of style, register, jargon, and slang are available within a language, and speakers may make choices according to their sense of the setting. Our words, phrases, and intonations will alter according to those present, to our desire to create or negate certain impressions, to our assessment of the desired level of formality, and so on. Across languages, code-switching is often more striking. One scholar wrote a paper titled "Sometimes I'll start a sentence in English *y terminó en español*."

Using words or terms from different languages in the same sentence or utterance has often been seen unfavorably, even by those who switch themselves: terms like Japlish, Franglais, and Spanglish are evidence here. Prejudice aside, however, it is hard to see that being able to draw upon double or triple pools of possibility—choosing the most apt or nuanced meaning, using a word from a second or third language to indicate particular emphasis or intimacy—is anything other than an expanded and useful capability.

Change: why and how?

There are still many things that are unclear about language variation and change, but questions of where it starts, and why, are central. Even minor alterations in words, sounds, and grammar can interfere with understanding, thus hindering communication. Some of the possible underpinnings of change have already been mentioned: contact between languages and communities is often key, particularly when one society is more dominant or more prestigious than another. On the other hand, isolation and lack of mobility can also bring about divergence; think again of the eventual fracturing of vulgar Latin. Needs change, too, making their impact felt particularly at the level of vocabulary.

In the broadest sense, the dynamics of group identity remain at center stage. Different languages mark communities or cultures or subcultures that wish to maintain some distinctiveness. Where groups share a language, distinctions are found at the dialectal level: Austrians are not Germans, Bolivians are not Spaniards, the Irish are not English. The sort of variation discussed in this chapter may represent part of ever-renewing processes of boundary marking. Change is sometimes ephemeral, and it may reflect unrealistic social and linguistic aspirations—but it may also be part of enduring changes in group identities. As Jack Chambers observed, "the underlying cause of sociolinguistic differences . . . is the human instinct to establish and maintain social identity."

Chapter 3
Perceptions of language

Attitudes are central to conceptions of identity: they reflect it and they help sustain it. Perceptions can often be deduced from behavior, but the relationship is not airtight. As well, assessing attitudes in a more focused way, or using them as part of decision-making processes is often important. Even if it does not correlate with action in neat ways, the assessment of attitudes can still be valuable. Disparities between people's attitudes (or reported attitudes) and their behaviors can sometimes be of particular interest. Since language characteristics often figure largely in our social and psychological perceptions, it is not surprising that attitudes and beliefs have been central to studies in the social life of language. Even though most of us would not venture an opinion on the state of string theory in physics, for example, few of us are without opinions about language. These opinions may be "amateur" views of language, but they often have immediate consequences in everyday life, regardless of their accuracy or sensitivity.

Strictly speaking, attitudes include cognitive, affective, and behavioral elements: that is, beliefs, emotions, and dispositions to act. There is often confusion between attitudes and beliefs, though, and this is not solely a popular misconception or inaccuracy. Many scholarly studies built upon responses to questionnaires or interviews claim to be reporting on attitudes when, in fact, they are only tapping beliefs. Yes-no answers to questions like "Is a knowledge of German important to you?" indicate only belief. Equating a yes with a favorable attitude might be incorrect, since such an answer *may* be based upon a grudging acceptance of the importance of German, which is, however, unaccompanied by much positive affect. An *attitude* measure here would clearly require further probing.

Beyond direct interviews, questionnaires, rating scales, and other pencil-and-paper methods, there are more indirect ways to assess reactions to language—that is to say, to speakers of particular varieties. For example, some studies have presented listeners with speakers of different language varieties, asking them for their evaluations along personality dimensions of interest: intelligence, humor, reliability, and so on. Other work has examined how listeners react to *supposedly* different speakers (reading the same neutral passage of prose, for instance, without variations of tone or emphasis). This "matched-guise" approach typically involves speakers who can create authentic versions of different accents or dialects. In a study conducted in Dublin, an actor from the Abbey Theatre produced educated middle-class versions of Galway, Cork, Cavan, Dublin, and Donegal accents. Providing the different "guises" are in fact native-like (something usually confirmed in pilot work), and providing the listener-judges don't guess that there is only one speaker (they typically don't), this method allows useful experimental control. Any idiosyncratic speech features that might confound listeners' evaluations of varieties produced by different speakers are obviously held constant here. The only thing that changes across guises is the speech variety.

A fairly consistent finding across many contexts is that speakers of standard dialects or of socially prestigious varieties are perceived in broadly favorable ways: they are seen as more competent and confident than others, and what they say is given greater weight. However, they need not be associated with the friendliness or trustworthiness that nonstandard speakers typically evoke. This surely mirrors real life and reminds us of the attractions of covert prestige.

Research has also shown that language evaluations can be associated with variables such as situation and context, speech rate, pitch, pausing, and intonation. In one set of studies, for instance, the least favorable judgments occurred when nonstandard accent, low lexical diversity, and working-class background were the interacting variables. In another study, using taped police interrogations, a speaker with a working-class Birmingham accent was rated significantly more guilty of the white-collar crime of check fraud than was an upper-middle-class speaker; the effect was magnified when the crime was armed robbery.

The bases of attitudinal judgment

Dictionary definitions of dialect and accent have often supported the popular view that nonstandard varieties are less correct than the "received" ones spoken by the socially dominant. But on what basis are evaluative judgments made? There are three broad possibilities, the first of which involves intrinsic linguistic differences. This view has had considerable historical support and remains common at an informal level in virtually all linguistically stratified societies. Nonetheless, scholarly research overwhelmingly rejects this possibility. Powerful evidence here emerged from Labov's work with urban varieties of African American English (AAE), sometimes referred to as "Ebonics." Coined in 1973 at a meeting of black scholars, this controversial term soon took on negative connotations—especially in the popular media—but it has since gained some favor within parts of the black community itself. AAE made an excellent test case since it had long been seen as a particularly deformed and unsystematic approximation to "good" English, and because its speakers were victims of a prejudice that went well beyond language alone. If it could be shown that AAE was not, after all, some debased variety, this would go some way toward establishing linguistic integrity for all dialect varieties.

Labov's work reinforced what casual observers had known for quite a long time: the vernacular black community is verbally rich, and, like "oral" cultures around the world, it supports and rewards those who are particularly linguistically gifted. Labov then demonstrated in clear and simple ways the grammatically rule-governed nature of AAE. As with all dialects, there are some variations. For instance, where standard English allows contraction of the copula verb ("He is going to work" can become "He's going to work"), AAE allows its deletion ("He going to work"—or, to include the most likely verb ending in this context, "He goin' to work"). This is a regular and not a random feature. Similarly, where standard English *does not* allow contraction ("He was going to work" cannot be simplified to "He's going to work"), AAE doesn't permit deletion. The reason is clear and has to do with avoiding confusion and ambiguity where past and present action is involved. But regularly allowing deletion in one variant, where contraction is the norm in the other, is simply to employ a different rule.

The reasonable extrapolation from such a useful test case is that *no* dialects are substandard, but some *are* nonstandard. If one variety is the standard in a particular context—spoken by educated people, used in writing—it logically follows that all other dialects must be nonstandard. This latter term is not pejorative in any technical linguistic sense. Neither AAE nor, by extension, any other nonstandard dialect can be characterized as some inaccurate and irregular poor cousin.

While nonstandard dialects are grammatically valid systems and not (at least, not in scholars' eyes and ears) deficient, some are perceived as more aesthetically appealing. Favorable attitudes *might* be reactions to varieties that are intrinsically more mellifluous. On the other hand, attractiveness might simply be a matter of personal preference: I find Italian the most beautiful language; you plump for Cantonese. In the 1930s, some scholars argued that RP was the "most pleasing and sonorous form" of English and, indeed, among the "most subtle and most beautiful of all expressions of the human spirit." Newspaper letters today reveal that many still feel the same way. A Canadian journalist's remarks—to the effect that dialect differences are just that— elicited strong responses from readers who felt that Canadian English should recall its superior British roots and resist the tide of American "slang." These are but contemporary examples of perceptions of linguistic strength, beauty, and expressivity that go back at least to Roman rhetoricians and grammarians like Quintilian and Priscian, and whose existence has remained strong throughout history. It is entirely understandable that some varieties have always been considered more honeyed than others, but is there any basis in fact for euphonic superiority?

It seems not. Modern study has compared the long-standing "inherent value" hypothesis here with one that suggests that all aesthetic judgments rest upon "imposed norms": certain varieties are heard as pleasant and cultured because of the status of their speakers. When English listeners who knew no Greek evaluated Athenian and Cretan varieties, no uniform aesthetic differences were detected; if anything, there was a tendency to hear the latter as more pleasant than the former. Of course, within the Greek speech community itself, the dialect of the capital is regularly judged as the most attractive. The implication is clear. When listeners are unaware of the powerful social connotations of dialects, when they are aware of nothing except the *sounds*, the aesthetic argument collapses. When the language *qua* language is all Greek to them . . .

Anyone who watches a film in which a woman dressed as a duchess speaks with a working-class accent can appreciate the point here. Nonnative speakers in the audience with a good understanding

35

of English, but not of dialect and class variation, could well miss a great deal of the comedic effect. The norms that produce that effect are "imposed" by community members in the know, and the stereotypes that link beauty, or harshness, or humor to a particular set of sounds are unavailable to others.

While listeners may *believe* that some varieties are grammatically or aesthetically superior to others, the evidence summarized here suggests otherwise. Once these two possibilities have been eliminated, the third and firmest basis of attitudinal evaluation emerges. The variant assessments found in the social laboratory and on the street reflect, above all, listeners' perceptions of the *speakers* of given varieties. The variety itself is a trigger or stimulus that evokes attitudes (or prejudices or stereotypes) about the community to which the speaker is thought to belong. It is useful to know this and to realize that there are no intrinsic grounds that elevate one variety over another, and to understand that social convention is the driving force here. Dialect difference and not relative deficiency is the issue. Equally, however, it is clear that society and not scholarship dictates here, that convention has always translated difference into deficit, and that social attitudes and stereotypes will not soon surrender to enlightened judgment.

Attitudes and alterations

It is hardly surprising that speakers of less prestigious nonstandard varieties come to feel the power of social convention, attitude, and prejudice—and, more than that, come to believe that it must in fact rest upon what is right and proper. Sociolinguists have thus described a "minority-group reaction" in which the codes, postures, and practices of the dominant become accepted and normative among the less dominant, even where they may coexist with class or group resentment. The linguist Michael Halliday wrote that "a speaker who is made ashamed of his own language habits suffers a basic injury as a human being," an assessment that is surely more poignant because the injury does not, as many continue to think, occur because of any substantive deficiencies.

Given the sturdiness of social prejudice and stereotype, the continued existence of low-status speech varieties might at first seem odd. If they are generally considered inferior, wouldn't more speakers try to eradicate them? And wouldn't shifting away from a language or, more likely, a dialect be a more popular option? There is ample evidence that such shifting is not an unattainable goal, and the ubiquity of the broadcast media today means that virtually everybody has at least a passive awareness of nonmaternal varieties. Indeed, some people *do* change, either completely replacing one variety with another, or expanding their linguistic repertoire to accommodate the requirements of different social contexts, thus becoming bilingual or bidialectal. So adaptations are possible.

These transitions are not without problems, however, and two come immediately to mind. First, it is no light matter to attempt alterations that will set you apart from members of your group: some severing of important ties may occur; you may be seen as a sort of pariah, resented or ostracized. Second, you must also hope that transitions come off successfully: falling between linguistic or cultural stools means risking social marginalization. Even relative success is tricky, particularly if you want to go home again. Mexican Americans who have "migrated" to English have been labeled *vendidos*, "sell-outs"; the same epithet has been applied to French Canadians, too: *vendus*. So, there are practical difficulties here, and this is even assuming that no other group markers (skin color, for instance) exist to hamper mobility.

The group-solidarity function of *any* variety can be compelling. A language variety of low social status may be a hindrance—a particularly unfair hindrance—but it is the variety of one's immediate group. The language of home and hearth, of first expression, of intimacy, is not abandoned or altered on a whim.

All varieties are capable of reflecting and sustaining bonds of the greatest significance, and language is clearly a potent support of personal group identity. It is true that identity can survive language shift, but it seems obvious that the expansion of linguistic repertoires, especially at the level of dialect, is an altogether more satisfactory adaptation than outright replacement. The implication is that, powerful social attitudes notwithstanding, language varieties of low prestige are unlikely to disappear. (And a good thing, too: they add their own particular flavor and value to the larger linguistic picture. All languages would be the poorer without the breadth of nuance found across the entire spectrum of class and regional variation.)

Studies of the perception of language varieties have taken into account many more variables than those described here. Over the last half-century, the use of a wide range of attitudinal (or belief) measures has produced a sizable literature. It is possible to predict with some confidence how people will react when they hear all sorts of dialect varieties, to understand why nonstandard speech can seem attractive to some middle-class speakers, to accept bilingual and bidialectal accommodations as entirely reasonable, and to assess reactions to the language of nonnative speakers. At a general level then, evaluative responses can be predicted quite well, as can the triggering of attitudes—often stereotypical ones— by variations in language and speech. The relationship between language and identity is not a mystery.

This sort of work has not gone very much beyond fairly gross explanations: it has done little to correlate speech evaluations with particular speech markers. Although hundreds of experiments have revealed negative reactions toward AAE, there is little formal information about the "triggering" role of particular pronunciation patterns, grammatical constructions, and vocabulary. On the other hand, more directly linguistic investigations *have* looked at features that characterize and differentiate language varieties: dialectal matters having to do with pronunciation (e.g., the nasality habitually associated with RP, or the presence or absence of postvocalic "r"); with grammar (deletion of the verb "to be" in African American English, or the use of double negatives); and, of course, with lexicon (I say *kerosene* and *gasoline*, you say *paraffin* and *petrol*).

Linguists have not been closely interested in relating such variations to differences in social ratings or have simply assumed that the more obvious and salient linguistic markers are the triggers for differentiated ratings. Their more socially minded colleagues, too, have generally been content to consider things

---

Box C
Copula deletion and double negatives

The now well-understood copula-deletion found in the Black English community is found among others, too. Many (white) people will have heard a policeman asking them, "That your car?"

Concerning double negatives: the Mrs. Grundys of the anglophone world have always told their pupils that it is logically incorrect to say something like "I don't have no bananas." The reasoning has as its first authority the eighteenth-century linguists Robert Lowth and Lindley Murray; they both argued that "two negatives in English destroy one another, or are equivalent to an affirmative." Contemporary Mrs. Grundys are making no allowance, of course, for the many dialects of English (Black English among them) in which the double-negative construction is a regular feature. The more enlightened would acknowledge, perhaps, that in some other *languages*, two negative markers do not turn verbs on their head: the French "ne . . . pas" construction is not a self-cancelling one. Discussing all this in class one day, a lecturer added that "There is, of course, no language in which a double positive makes a negative." Comes a sardonic voice from the back of the room, "Yeah! Right!"

at the "macro" level, and to accept that describing perceptions evoked by identifiable speech patterns is sufficient: I hear someone speak, I realize the person is from Texas (or Tyneside), and a connected and predictable set of reactions follow. While there have been some notable exceptions in both the linguistic and the social camps, it is obvious that more bridging efforts could refine and particularize our knowledge of how *specific* aspects of speech elicit *specific* types of evaluative assessments. One might think that beyond specialized academic interest there is little need for such fine-grained knowledge. After all, most of the stimuli are embedded in a host of class or ethnic markers, and stereotypic reactions are gross and general by definition. Even very limited stimuli can evoke quite marked reactions, however.

Some have suggested that the whole focus on language attitudes is broadly misplaced, on the grounds that necessity, real or perceived, typically overpowers attitude in real-life settings. It is certainly the case that most historical changes in language use owe much more to socioeconomic and political pressures than they do to attitudes per se. But perhaps attitudes of a sort *are* important in large-scale linguistic dynamics, in the shift that moves a group from one language to another. A mid-nineteenth-century Irishman may have hated English and what it represented, while still acknowledging the pragmatic value of the language. Perhaps a useful distinction might be drawn between *positive* and *favorable* attitudes. Perhaps Irish attitudes toward learning English were positive in an instrumental sense but not necessarily favorable or "integrative"—a term that refers to aspirations that go beyond language-as-tool, perhaps to wholehearted desires to join another culture.

There is an interesting educational aspect here, too. While a common criticism of language classrooms is that they often remain detached from any real-world nexus of language and culture, attitudes might in fact assume particular importance in such settings. That is, where a context is *not* perceived to be immediately pertinent to (or reflective of) current concerns—where, for example, classroom French is not studied for practical or instrumental reasons—attitudes may make a real difference. In some circumstances, then, the importance of favorable attitudes may vary inversely with linguistic necessity.

An important and burgeoning literature, one that rests upon attitudes and perceptions, has to do with the accommodations made by speakers in different contexts and with different intentions. Adaptations can take many forms, but, whether operating at or below the level of conscious awareness, the fundamental feature is the modification of speech patterns to converge with or diverge from those of others. Accommodation can reflect individual concerns, such as wanting to sound more like the boss or departing from the usage of someone you dislike. It can also highlight group concerns: one may wish to stress "in-group" membership or to solidify an ethnic or class boundary. Work in this "psychology of dialogue" can be seen as a general manifestation of the more recent and more detailed interest in conversation and discourse analysis.

Discourse analysis

With the study of conversation and discourse, as well as with ever-closer text analysis, an important focus on more fine-grained language matters has emerged in recent decades. The obvious link to perceptions and attitudes arises here because of the central thrust in all such work—the production and interpretation of social meaning. And this, in turn, almost immediately highlights variations in speaker status and power. Whether formal or informal, conscious or not, the manipulation of language in all "speech acts" emerges from attitudinal bases and provokes specific perceptions in the ears of listeners or the eyes of readers. One commentator refers to such study, in its "critical" clothing, as "discourse analysis with attitude." *All* such study, of course, has attitude.

The sociologist Harold Garfinkel's "ethnomethodology" aimed to elucidate the detailed ways in which we produce social meanings: How do we define ourselves? How do we understand and influence the many situations in which we find ourselves? How do we construe our relations with others? In its broadest sense—and ethnomethodology is nothing if not broad—the term suggests a sociology that makes room for contextually rich, even phenomenological, approaches and interpretations. As a linguistic arm of ethnomethodology, "conversation analysis" was an obvious necessity. Indeed, nothing is more central to the understanding of human social interaction than language.

Conversation analysis is all about how talk works: it attends principally to such matters as the initiation and termination of interchanges, the rules and practices governing turn-taking, interruptions and interjections, the appropriate sequencing of argument, the perils of miscommunication and their rectification, and the appropriateness of topics and styles of discussion. Embracing but going beyond investigations of naturally occurring speech, the more expansive discourse analysis concerns itself with context and, above all with the power relationships that stand behind and emerge within all linguistic events, spoken or written. Discourse analysis has given much attention, then, to political language and to other social arenas (law, medicine, education, media, and popular culture) in which language and status differences figure importantly. In what can be called a linguistic ethnography, "language and the social world are mutually shaping" and close attention to "situated language use" is therefore called for. While not exactly novel ideas, these are nevertheless welcome observations, given the regrettable gaps within and among psychology, sociology, and linguistics.

Triangulated approaches to language use recommend themselves in many settings. In classrooms, for instance, closer analysis of teacher-pupil interactions, and greater awareness of cross-cultural and cross-dialectal differences can be very useful. Recent Canadian work has shown that teachers typically dominate the "linguistic space" in the classroom to an overwhelming degree and, of the small portion available to the pupils, boys often claim the lion's share: one study found the ratio of girls' to boys' verbal contributions to be on the order of 1:10. Earlier studies revealed that American Indian children often fell foul of their teachers, who viewed their reluctance to speak in class as reflections of sullenness or shyness, who often felt that the cultures from which they came were deficient, who sometimes even associated taciturnity with cognitive backwardness. These are all quite unwarranted conclusions, arising from inadequate understanding of differing cultural injunctions that bear upon speech in public, in front of peers, and when confronted with authority figures.

Problems with discourse analysis and its associated fields

Ethnomethodological inquiry is theoretically so broad in its remit that any disciplinary precision is essentially unattainable. Perhaps because of this, ethnomethodology and allied undertakings became more like sects or cliques, closed systems in which members talk to other members, where insights exist that are denied to outsiders (as Lewis Coser put it in his 1975 presidential address to the American Sociological Association). A reviewer of Garfinkel's "seminal" text succinctly observed that ethnomethodology involved "an extraordinarily high ratio of reading time to information transfer."

Similarly, discourse analysis and the many "critical" sub-areas with which it is often associated have become increasingly narrow or inward-looking. An important example here is provided by "critical discourse analysis," the main interests of which lie in "political discourse, media, advertisement, ideology, racism [and] institutional discourse." Clearly positioning itself to be timely and relevant, this analysis is not an ideologically neutral enterprise and is, indeed, "upfront about its own, explicitly left-wing, political commitment." It is "discourse analysis with attitude." There are dangers, of course, when relatively disinterested work is mixed with special pleading. Henry Widdowson points to specific difficulties when he writes that critical discourse analysis often departs from "the conventions of rationality, logical consistency, empirical substantiation and so on."

An intrinsic difficulty with discourse analysis has to do with the selection of particular speech and language samples from larger ongoing "interactions": there is an infinity of choice here. As contemporary journal articles abundantly illustrate, choices are frequently made without any compelling justification, raising questions of "representativeness, selectivity, partiality, prejudice, and voice." One of the consequences would seem to be a potentially endless series of fact-gathering exercises.

Observers have also noted the difficulties in a field where the explanations can be so much more detailed (and take up so much more space) than the phenomena under study. An egregious example is found in a study that devoted more than six hundred pages to an analysis of a committee's evaluation of a doctoral dissertation. The actual transcript analyzed was less than three hundred lines of text, representing about ten minutes of conversation among four examiners. This study is clearly a great improvement on Borges's famous map of the world on a scale of 1:1: here there is the potential for a map of the sociolinguistic world many times larger than the actual world itself. Even so, the author of the study later admitted that neither a "comprehensive discourse analysis" nor a "unified theory of sociolinguistic description" was produced, and even suggested that such an analysis was a chimera. Finally, a reviewer acknowledged (how could he not?) that the study had shown how much can be derived from so little—but ended with the comment that "for students of spoken interaction, such an experience confirms what is already known." *Parturiunt montes; nascetur ridiculus mus*— mountainous labor gives birth to a silly little mouse.

The general area has also become a volatile one with much internal wrangling, an instance, perhaps, of the dictum that academic infighting is so vicious because the stakes are so low. Unsurprisingly, there is much jargon while, at the same time, the work often alternates between the obvious and the impenetrable. Lewis Coser has also remarked on the curious tendency (not limited to ethnomethodologists) for those professionally interested in language and communication to be such poor communicators themselves. Meant to overturn sterile social-scientific empiricism and narrow positivism, discourse analysis and its offshoots have increasingly become introverted and isolated enterprises. Like a game of chess (but more elaborate, in that there are infinite possibilities for redefinition and realignment of the rules), they are fascinating to their players but usually quite divorced from the social reality that should be both their base and the recipient of their insights.

In various guises and emphases, discourse analysis remains popular in many circles. It has done its practitioners some considerable good, at least within the inbred confines that they increasingly inhabit, but without creating breakthroughs of any significance for the intended beneficiaries. Most of the work, of most social scientists, most of the time, makes very little direct contribution toward the societies within which it operates, of course. But we should be particularly careful when considering areas whose very existence is based upon the desire to produce applicable results, whose findings are generally gathered "in the field"—but whose sense of that field is restricted, and whose production of jargon and neologism increases at a geometric pace. Good and useful language analysis has been done under a number of headings, and more is doubtless to come. There is some promise, but at the moment the area is essentially an incestuous preserve of little applied value.

Chapter 4
Protecting language

Like most enquiries, scientific or informal, interest in the
language-and-society relationship has typically involved
comparison and categorization; these often lead to assessments
of quality. Although "purism" and "prescriptivism" are terms
suggesting judgmental stances that are no longer seen as
correct in many quarters, they still enjoy vigorous life in
others. While not all linguistic purism is silly and not all
prescriptivism unnecessary, the contemporary scholarly distaste
for prescriptivism must be acknowledged. This distaste is partly
based upon the entirely fallacious notion that to study something
is to endorse it; it also ignores a mundane prescriptivism to
which we all attend.

Roughly speaking, linguistic *prescriptivism* reflects the idea
that language standards must be maintained and that unwanted
influences are to be resisted. (*Purism* is the term sometimes
preferred where undesirable *foreign* influence is concerned.) In
the European context, important prescriptivist impulses were a
consequence of the decline of Latin and the ascent of European
national languages. With the latter came the association between
cultural and linguistic specificity, and from this there inexorably
emerged the desire to preserve and protect what was increasingly
seen as an important boundary marker. Contemporary
manifestations include francophone attempts to keep English at

bay, worries about language "decline," complaints about the rising tide of slang, and concerns for "correctness."

Linguistic prescriptivism has traditionally figured importantly in the work of academicians and lexicographers charged with linguistic regularization of one sort or another. A standardizing language, especially in the age of print, requires some "normalization," but this means making choices that will strengthen some dialects and weaken others—part of the process that separates standard from nonstandard dialects. Furthermore, there have always been questions about the *extent* of prescriptivism, coupled with a sense that, ultimately, "ordinary" usage will prevail.

Formal prescriptivist interventions typically arose to deal with the need for language regularization created by technological advance, increasing literacy, and swelling conceptions of national solidarity. Consider William Caxton, who had to make a selection from varying English dialects because of the imperatives of printing. In his prologue to *Eneydos*—a version of the *Aeneid*—published in 1490, he muses on change:

> And certaynly our language now vsed varyeth ferre from that whiche was vsed and spoken when I was borne . . . and that comyn englysshe that is spoken in one shyre varyeth from a nother . . . it is harde to playse euery man by cause of dyuersite and chaunge of langage.

In his *Ars Poetica*, Horace encouraged careful and direct writing, and the avoidance of purple prose, suggesting that words come and go as ordinary usage dictates. Just over a century later, Quintilian wrote in his *Institutio Oratoria* (ca. 100 CE) that linguistic correctness was ultimately linked to public usage. He seemed, then, to agree with Horace, advocating linguistic *descriptivism* rather than prescriptivism or purism. However, like many similar commentators since then, Quintilian had a rather limited public in mind: he meant the *educated* public, not the masses whose language was full of "barbarisms" (a Greek word, incidentally, signifying stammering). Fifteen centuries later, the French grammatician Vaugelas grudgingly accepted that popular usage ultimately reigns; he noted, however, that only the best representatives of the aristocracy and the authors of the day should be standard-setters.

In practice, the reasonable requirement of accepted standards was ever intertwined with notions of correctness, implying the necessity of educated choice. The work of national language academies and councils has always been dominant here, and the Académie française is the single best example: in 1635, Cardinal Richelieu gave it "absolute power . . . over literature and language." There are always forty members of the academy—predominantly writers and other scholars—whose job it is to oversee and regulate the development and the integrity of French. As with similar bodies elsewhere, their efforts have not always been very successful, either in their grammatical and lexical productions or, more specifically, in their attempts to intervene in the dynamics of language use. But this hardly detracts from their importance as manifestations of will and intent, nor does it vitiate their sociological and political role as protectors of group identity. Whether self-appointed or recipients of royal accolade, the protectionist impulses of academicians have usually been able to rely upon broad popular support (if not understanding).

The sentiments of language conservatives are generally widely endorsed, remain potent in the general imagination, and account for the numerous style manuals, language handbooks, vade mecums, and, of course, the frequent eruptions in the popular press. While often railing against unwanted foreign incursions, many historical guides to "correct" grammar, vocabulary, and usage focused upon provincialisms, generally seen as threats to linguistic unity and hindrances to standardized practice. In eighteenth-century France, for example, the vernaculars of

Sociolinguistics

48

4. The Académie française is the oldest of the five bodies making up the Institut de France. The view here is from the pedestrian bridge that links the Institut and the Louvre.

Gascony, Flanders, and Provence came in for the greatest censure. The broad and unflagging popularity of language handbooks in the anglophone world is demonstrated not only by their numbers but also by the variations of depth that they have offered: the serious undertakings of Henry Fowler, Ernest Gowers, Robert Burchfield, and others have been matched in our own time by the altogether lighter and more personal treatments of Kingsley Amis, Simon Winchester, Bill Bryson, and Jean Aitchison. They all, it seems, have linguistic axes to grind.

Influential writers and public figures have long written about linguistic decline and decay, identified the chief malefactors, and suggested what ought to be done: there has never been a shortage of "amateur do-gooding missionaries." But not every critic has been animated by religious zeal. George Orwell's several essays on language come to mind, but there are many other thoughtful discussions—not narrow woe-is-me treatments of rot and ruin but more measured criticism of deliberate or ignorant misuse, of unnecessary neologism, of jargon and propaganda.

At more rarefied levels, prescriptivism has become a four-letter word, with scholars arguing that it is neither desirable nor feasible to attempt to intervene in the "natural" life of language. A deliberate renunciation of prescriptivism is more like atheism than agnosticism: a conscious nonbelief is, itself, a belief, and a refusal to intervene is essentially prescriptivism in reverse. In any event, in their rush away from prescriptivism, linguists may have abdicated a useful role as arbiters and may have left much of the field open to those styled as "language shamans" by Dwight Bolinger, one of the few linguists who was willing to write about the "public life" of language. Bolinger rightly criticized the obvious crank elements, but he also understood the desire, however ill-informed, for authoritative standards.

Prescriptivism and planning

In his 1712 *Proposal for Correcting, Improving and Ascertaining the English Tongue*, Jonathan Swift rebelled against the "infusion of enthusiastick jargon," against the corrupting "licentiousness" of the Restoration. He called for "eminent persons" to form a society, perhaps along the lines of the Académie française. Opinions for and against a prescriptivist institution continued (and are still expressed today), but no government-sponsored English-language academy has ever appeared—not in England, not in America, not in any other anglophone country. (An English academy *was* established in South Africa in 1961, but it lacks an official imprimatur.) This is an anomaly in a world where the great majority of countries (and often regions) have language-planning bodies. There are at least one hundred such institutions currently in existence, and several have important subcategories, such as the eight or nine Arabic academies or the twenty or so Spanish-language bodies.

Anglophones on each side of the Atlantic did not dismiss the needs and the pleas for standards. Rejecting the academy approach that was so common throughout Europe and beyond—and perhaps *because* it was so common elsewhere—both Britain and America opted for one-man institutions. In England, Samuel Johnson's great dictionary appeared in 1755. Earlier, Johnson had adopted a "purifying" posture, but he became more descriptivist (if sometimes grudgingly so), rejecting any attempt at "embalming" a language and implying that attempts to arrest linguistic change were ill-advised.

Inheriting the British linguistic tradition meant that the newly independent United States also inherited an ambivalent attitude toward prescriptivism. While some—most notably John Adams— argued for a formal institution to stem linguistic "degeneration," a proposition generally felt to reveal elite or monarchist sympathies was unlikely to attract much support. Hence the American one-man academy in the form of Noah Webster, whose dictionary was published in 1828. Like Johnson, he saw that the "force of common usage" was not to be resisted. And, like Johnson, he also hoped to discourage "improprieties and vulgarisms," as well as the "odious distinctions of provincial dialects." Unlike Johnson, however, Webster believed that his work could divide as well as unify, the division here being that between English and American usage: national identity again. In his lexicography, Webster wanted to take a shared language and give it some distinctive American clothing. Some of his innovations took root: *color* for *colour*, *center* for *centre*, *traveling* for *travelling*, and so on; other suggestions fared less well (*tung* and *thum*, for example). He also made careful room in his dictionary for native words (*skunk*, *moose*, *succotash*).

The work of lexicographers, then and now, clearly illustrates an ongoing tension between descriptivism and prescriptivism. Even the most "inclusive" treatments, even the most widely cast of linguistic nets, must involve choice. Beyond standardization and normalization, the efforts of individuals and committees have also always been in the service of national solidarity. As Bishop Thomas Wilson wrote in 1724, "a good language . . . is both an Honour and of great Use to a Nation," thereby endorsing language as both instrument and symbol. Webster looked forward to an eventual linguistic schism, on the grounds that a country that had broken free from its origins ought to have its own language. Johnson's rather muscular sense of English national pride appeared once more in James Murray's nineteenth-century *Oxford English Dictionary*. The linguist Max Müller saw it as a patriotic endeavor engaging the "national honour" of England.

Considering the linguistically standardizing aspects of the great English dictionaries, but also bearing in mind the importance of the relationship between language and group identity, it is clear that the current global scope of English has complicated matters in interesting ways. In a world of "Englishes," with many regional varieties and local standards, perceptions of the "ownership" of English are rapidly changing. The bedrock authority of the old native speakers in England and, later, in America remained unquestioned for a long time, but now the presence of millions of newer native speakers, mainly in countries of what was the British Empire—as well as those millions more who have added English to their language repertoires—means that contemporary prescriptivist intentions, needs, and interventions have become multifaceted.

In earlier times, scholars were the prescriptivists, but it is now the man or woman in the street (or in the newspaper) who is likely to rail against change, unwanted influence, and degeneration, to cry out for correctness, authority, and the maintenance of standards. Prescriptivist stances are not wholly foreign to the contemporary scholarly community, however, since issues of language "management" remain important. All of the many and varied undertakings of language planners are necessarily prescriptivist to some degree, since all presuppose intentions and desired outcomes. Whether it is constructing new or revised orthographies, choosing among dialects, or implementing spelling reform, all planning is inevitably colored by ideological imperatives. There are disinterested theories of language planning, to be sure, but application immediately involves opinion and preference, and what appears as desirable progress to some may be persecution to others. Some of the most dramatic instances are those in which the demands of identity are allowed to trump communicative practicality, such as in the case of Serbo-Croatian.

A final point here: any desire to intervene in behalf of endangered languages—a desire that has now become attractive to many within and without the academy—implies a willingness to engage in prescriptivist exercises. This is an interesting conundrum for those whose liberal impulses generally embrace both a concern for the "small," the "authentic," and the "threatened," and a dislike of "interfering" in other cultures.

Prescriptivism did not, could not, and ought not to have come to an end with the advent of modern linguistic insight. Some exercises in what Deborah Cameron calls "verbal hygiene" may be decried, but certainly not all of them. On the one hand, prescriptivism and purism based upon narrow and often unfair conceptions of social inclusion and exclusion; on the other, justifiable planning in behalf of broadly desirable normalization. The tension here is a permanent one.

In short, all language planning is prescriptive; while some is indefensibly narrow and partisan, that which occurs under most scholarly auspices is more justifiable. It can take a number of important forms. Determining which variety will be given some sort of official or national standing reflects outright language choice. Language standardization (for the emerging national European varieties, for instance) may be required. Writing systems may have to be developed, grammars may require regularization, vocabularies may need expansion and modernization. These activities have been formalized in the literature as language selection, codification, implementation, and elaboration; the first two comprise "status planning," the latter two "corpus planning." The purely linguistic aspects (codification and elaboration) are less central than the social ones (selection and implementation). Academic language planners essentially engage in technical activities and, while these obviously involve real expertise, they typically occur *after* the central decisions have been taken by others: the politicians and administrators, the captains and the kings. Although he was talking about rationalizing language borders in particular, the words of Elie Kedourie—the famous scholar of nationalism—are broadly applicable here. He wrote that it is "absurd to think that professors of linguistics and collectors of folklore can do the work of statesmen and soldiers. What does happen is that academic enquiries are used by conflicting interests to bolster up their claims, and their results prevail only to the extent that somebody has the power to make them prevail."

The ecology of language

Current interest in the "ecology of language" is a specific development under the broad rubric of "language planning." Meaningful treatments of the social life of language have always attended to the necessary contextualization, and careful scholars were always ecologically minded *avant la lettre*. Despite the breadth implied in the term, contemporary work under the ecological heading has often become a narrowed planning variant that focuses upon the threats to endangered languages. This is not to suggest that all modern work in language planning now takes place under this particular heading, but the "new" ecology of language does seem to be increasingly attractive. It thus makes for a useful object lesson, one that touches upon many important strands, reveals several serious shortcomings, and should be of interest to general readers and students alike.

When the subdiscipline was first popularized in the 1970s, language ecology had a breadth of vision meant to embrace *all* linkages among languages and their environments, and to counter any tendencies to think about language in isolated or stand-alone fashion. Its scope has, however, progressively shrunk. Now a growing segment of the literature concerns itself chiefly with the maintenance of linguistic diversity, which is seen as an unalloyed good, to be defended wherever it seems to falter. While a truly ecological perspective would take into account all sorts of relationships and outcomes, from ruddy linguistic health all the way to extinction, the modern variant now argues for a kinder, gentler nexus. As the ecolinguist Peter Mühlhäusler recently noted, "functioning ecologies are nowadays characterized by predominantly mutually beneficial links and only to a small degree by competitive relationships." This seems an unwarranted limitation since, like all others, linguistic environments are often harsh or indifferent. Big and small languages, for instance, often have a less than pacific relationship, one that recalls to mind Woody Allen's reworking of a passage from Isaiah: "the lion and the calf shall lie down together, but the calf won't get much sleep."

A preference for diversity, linguistic and otherwise, is common; indeed, it is difficult to imagine that any educated perspective would vote for monotony over color, for sameness over variety. This does not imply that the idea that linguistic diversity is always a good and valuable thing must never be questioned. Nor should scholars shy away from full and dispassionate consideration of the conditions necessary for diversity to thrive. One might be more indulgent toward the limitations of the formal shortcomings of the contemporary ecology of language if it expanded earlier insights and suggested novel ways to maintain at-risk languages. In fact, these shortcomings serve only to highlight difficulties that have been quite well understood for some time. Archival embalming apart, most can be summarized by observing that the maintenance of languages involves much more than language alone. Acknowledgment of this suggests the scope of the difficulties commonly encountered.

"Language loss" is something of a misnomer. Although varieties have certainly disappeared, their *speakers* never lack communicative skills: during the shift from one medium to another, very few individuals actually say nothing. But the idea of some absolute loss typically underpins arguments in support of the maintenance of diversity. It is curious to decry the passing of "ancestral cultures, as if cultures were static systems and the emergence of new ones in response to changing ecologies was necessarily maladaptive" (as Salikoko Mufwene recently pointed out). Such a nondynamic point of view is surely ironic from an ecological perspective, and it reflects the mistaken sense that "only one language can best mirror or convey a particular culture."

A recent argument in the language-ecology literature has compared language and biological diversity. Since most would agree that diversity of all stripes can contribute to a richer and more nuanced world, the connection is interesting—at a metaphorical level. If we intervene to save snails and whales, to maintain historic buildings, and to preserve rare literary and cultural artifacts, should we not also attempt to stem language decline and to prevent larger languages from swallowing smaller ones? In fact, some have argued that the connection is more than metaphorical, and that linguistic and biological diversity are *actually* connected. This is a dubious argument. There is, in any event, a practical problem: it is more difficult to save languages than to save species. The preservation of flora and fauna is hard enough, of course but, still, with sufficient will we can exercise a degree of control that, short of dictatorial imposition, is impossible with human cultures and languages.

Those interested in ecolinguistics have often pointed an accusing finger at human actions that have upset previously balanced ecologies. In what sphere, however, has human "interference" *not* altered things? What social spheres could there possibly be *without* such actions? It seems like lamenting the fact that we have two ears. The curiously static quality of much ecological thinking comes to mind here: the implication often seems to be that, once some cultural and linguistic balance is achieved, some wrong righted and some redress made, new arrangements will remain in place forever. Again, this is naive.

Part of the ideological underpinning of language ecology in its contemporary manifestations is a distrust of literacy and education on the grounds that they often undercut the preservation of linguistic diversity. Indeed, scholars sometimes argue that literacy promotion actually works against "linguistic vitality." Just as large languages are villains, so written varieties can push oral ones aside, erasing the traditional knowledge they bear. Literacy is also seen as a sort of Trojan horse, with speakers of endangered languages lulled into a false sense of security once writing arrives. It is true that literacy does not inevitably lead to social or political improvement, but it would surely be dangerous to try and purchase language maintenance at the expense of literacy.

A related suggestion is that formal education is not always the ally of enduring diversity, since it too has intrusive qualities. Not only does formal education champion literacy over orality, it often imposes foreign (read "Western") values and methods upon small cultures. It is not difficult to sympathize with laments about cultural intrusion, but *all* thoroughgoing education is multicultural in nature, expanding local horizons and crossing national and disciplinary boundaries. The difficulties besetting small languages will not be significantly countered by trying to keep the world at bay. Where languages in contact are of unequal clout, education will necessarily provide evidence of disparities. In reasonably democratic settings, it reflects more than it causes.

The modern ecological perspective is a romanticized one. Just as eighteenth-century romanticism was a reaction to the Enlightenment, so there is now a disparagement of the scientific culture and the "privileging" of its knowledge over "folk wisdom." There is a special regard for small cultures and local knowledges, and it takes two forms. The first is a simple and perfectly reasonable desire for the survival of such cultures and systems. The second argues that their conduct and their values are superior to those of larger societies; this view is generally expressed in some muted fashion, but occasionally the mask slips. Thus, Tapani Salminen has argued that "without romanticizing or idealizing the indigenous cultures, it is clear that they are superior to the mass culture because their members retain the capability of living in at least relative harmony with the natural environment." Despite the disclaimer, this *is* romanticism, as is the recent book dedication by Luisa Maffi: "to the world's indigenous and traditional peoples, who hold the key to the inextricable link between [*sic*] language, knowledge and the environment."

A dislike of the contemporary world, a "pronounced anti-globalisation, anti-Western and anti-Cartesian" stance—as Frank Polzenhagen and René Dirven have put it—often forms the background for arguments on behalf of small cultures and stands at the center of a romanticized ecology-of-language model.

Contemporary language ecology often argues that all people have the *right* to maintain and use their native language, and that groups, organizations, and governments have an obligation to respect and encourage the exercise of this right. While it is possible to legislate rights of language expression, it is rather more difficult to legislate rights to be understood, and formal protection of use is rather hollow if, in the public and unofficial areas of life where languages really rise or fall, it has little or no communicative value.

There are deeper issues, too. The most pivotal has to do with whether rights exist at all. Perhaps there are no inherent rights, perhaps there are only assertions—and perhaps what we have come to accept as human rights are assertions that have been widely endorsed and then protected in law. In any event, current emphases upon "language rights" generally remain at the level of assertion, and it is disingenuous to imply that *claims* are sufficient to somehow give such rights the same strength of footing as those now underpinned by criminal or civil codes. To put it another way: while legally protected rights imply moral assertions, the reverse does not necessarily hold. (What is merely desirable today may of course become lawfully codified tomorrow.) Language rights are also typically discussed in relation to groups, and this can sit uneasily with traditional liberal-democratic principles that enshrine rights in individuals. Some political philosophers— including Will Kymlicka, Alan Patten, and Philippe van Parijs— have begun to look more closely at this distinction, but their nuanced inquiries are rarely understood in the language-ecology literature.

In short, much of the current work in the ecology of language reflects a particular sociopolitical ideology, one aimed at the maintenance of linguistic diversity, the encouragement of language learning, and the endorsement of language rights; these are all facets of a resistance to big languages generally and to English specifically. An activist role is implied in Mühlhäusler's argument for scholars to be "shop stewards for linguistic diversity." None of this suggests, of course, that linguists and others must renounce personal opinion and aspiration. None of it suggests that the case for language diversity has no basis. Quite the contrary. It is misleading, though, to present a very specific set of arguments under the very general heading of language ecology. It is also misleading to claim that these arguments are the only ones open to enlightened opinion when they rest, in fact, upon particular perceptions of morality and aesthetic preference.

Chapter 5
Languages great and small

The idea that some languages are better than others has a long history. In his great scientific poem, *De rerum natura* (ca. 55 BCE), Lucretius refers several times to the insufficiencies of Latin, to the difficulties of representing in it the Greek theories and discoveries he wishes to elucidate for his readers, to his sense of being thwarted by the poverty of "our native tongue." He may, indeed, have been at least partly right: one of his contemporary translators observed that, in comparison to the Greeks, the Romans were

> a semi-barbarous people who had displayed unequalled aptitude
> for the arts of government and war but had so far devoted very little
> thought to "the nature of the universe." The Latin of Lucretius's
> day had no accepted philosophic or scientific vocabulary, and his
> generation had to create one for themselves on the Greek model.

This underpinning of Lucretius's laments is also somewhat wrong, however, and on several counts. First, among the cognoscenti the knowledge of the Greeks was available via the Greek language itself: Greek was the Latin of its day, the scholarly lingua franca. Second, the Latin of Lucretius was not quite so intellectually barren as the translator suggests, nor was it quite the medium of a "semi-barbarous" people. Third, and relatedly, his acknowledgment of the growth of new vocabulary underscores a vital point made earlier (about dialects). While not all varieties are equally developed across their entire range, they are adequate for the existing needs of their speakers. As these needs change—but only then—languages can be expected to change, too: they all have the potential for virtually limitless alteration and expansion.

Most language comparisons have of course pitted one's own superior variety against lesser lights. The sixteenth-century Holy Roman Emperor Charles V thought that Spanish was the only language suitable for discussions about (and with) divinity, and that Italian and French were suitable for ordinary conversations. German was a much cruder medium, however; the emperor said that he spoke it to his horses. Two centuries later, when visiting the royal court in Berlin, Voltaire found a similar linguistic distribution: as in the rest of European high society, French was the prestigious language there; German was "pour les soldats et pour les chevaux" (for soldiers and horses).

In the early seventeenth century, Richard Carew, an English antiquary, wrote that Italian was "pleasant, but without sinews"; French "delicate, but ever nice as a woman"; Spanish "majestical but fulsome"; and Dutch "manlike, but withal very harsh." None could compare to the overall "excellency" of English. And there are the even more familiar remarks of Antoine de Rivarol, in the late eighteenth century. French, he said, was synonymous with clarity of expression and meaning; indeed, "ce qui n'est pas clair n'est pas français"—English and other languages were, however, mediums of ambiguity. George Lemon, a clergyman and a teacher, disdained all others in comparison with "the purity and dignity, and all the high graceful majesty" of eighteenth-century English. In the mid-nineteenth century, the American diplomat and linguist George Marsh wrote that English was "emphatically the language of commerce, of civilisation, of social and religious freedom, of progressive intelligence, and of an active catholic philanthropy." At the same time, Edward Higginson, a cleric who dabbled in philology—as so many reverend gentlemen seemed to do—wrote that "there is not, nor ever was, a language comparable to the English."

These and the great many other similar sentiments are entirely predictable. Group identity requires boundaries, preferably ones to be proud of, and expressions of linguistic exclusivity can buttress them. In and of themselves, these comments are inaccurate and ludicrous, but they are socially revealing. Specifically, they highlight a pride in cultural and linguistic dominance that no doubt seemed imperishable. In many contemporary eyes, the eclipse of English is also hard to imagine: its global penetration is unmatched and its progress relentless. Indeed, it has advantages denied to earlier lingua francas. Historical precedent would have suggested that the decline of British power meant the decline of English, but waiting in the wings was an English-speaking America. And even if others, including the "BRIC" countries (Brazil, Russia, India, and China), are now readying themselves to overtake American dominance, English may find its lease extended once again as the new economies continue to use the language of wider communication to which they have all become so thoroughly accustomed. If so, we could have a historically odd situation in which changes in regional power and prestige might *not* imply changes in existing language fortunes.

English was once a small language. The French that came to England with the Norman Conquest was both an invading language and the marker of status and prestige. Thus, in the thirteenth century, Robert of Gloucester observed that "vor bote a man conne Frenss me telþ of him lute / ac lowe men holdeþ to Engliss." In other words, unless a man knows French, people pay him little heed; and only "low men" keep to English. Even allowing for its resilience in the face of Norman French, English remained small. French, Spanish, and Italian were the powerful international varieties, widely studied in Tudor and Stuart England. Queen Elizabeth was only the most prominent among many language students.

While later developments would put English in the ascendant, as late as the early seventeenth century its position gave little hint of future global status. With four or five million speakers, it remained of limited importance, well back in the linguistic sweepstakes. It is all too easy, today, to forget the historical vicissitudes of English. Its strength and scope may be greater than those of previous lingua francas, but the differences are ones of degree, not of principle. Anglophones ought not to be glib, of course, nor should they imagine that historical insights need lessen the impact of English upon other varieties. The anxieties felt by those whose languages and cultures exist in the shadow of larger neighbors have always been real enough. Still, this is a very old drama we are looking at here, one whose plot endures while the cast changes: some eternal *Mousetrap*.

Imperialism and endangerment

It has been suggested that the rapidity and the extent of the spread of English has been considerably assisted by anglophone governments and their servants. This alleged "linguistic imperialism" is seen as the main motor of "linguicism." There always has been linguistic discrimination, of course, and the deliberate banning of certain varieties in certain contexts is not only an historical matter (nor, of course, has it always involved English). Nonetheless, the idea that some hegemonical impulse is key to the spread of the language is too tidy and too narrow a view. For activists and, indeed, for some disinterested language scholars, acknowledging the prepotent unofficial forces behind English—influences that pull as well as push the language—means accepting an inconvenient truth.

English does seem to spread ever wider, pushing less dominant varieties aside, but the process is rarely conspiratorial. Defenders and promoters of interests to which the growth of English contributes will certainly support the language, and anglophone foreign policy—through the workings of bodies like the British Council—encourages and welcomes its global reach. Such conscious support is hardly vital, however. The powerful unofficial pressures that emanate from political, economic, and cultural dominance, and which have always led people to the linguistic Rome of the day, are quite sufficient to explain the current status of English. Without them, formal policies would be both silly and impotent. (By the way, France has its *Alliance française*, Portugal its *Instituto Camões*, Italy the *Società Dante Alighieri*, and Germany the *Goethe-Institut*: a sampling of the many national bodies established to promote language and culture. The impulse is a natural one.)

Sociolinguistics

An important aspect of the imperialism thesis is that powerful languages have been shoved down the throats of subordinate populations who are easily manipulated and whose best interests have been overridden. Again, however, this is neither a parsimonious nor a particularly plausible thesis. Groups around the world are not merely passive recipients of English today, and it is interesting that those who argue against the iniquities of linguistic imperialism seem, themselves, to be patronizing in implying lack of "agency" among the millions of people learning English around the world. Sir Shridath Ramphal, a former secretary-general of the Commonwealth, wrote in 1996 that while the history behind the spread of English is not always one to be proud of, the linguistic legacy is now of use to all. The sociologist Joshua Fishman, no fan of big languages, reports that interactions between English and other varieties do not highlight imperialism but, rather, practical aspirations, often resulting in linguistic divisions of labor. As another scholar has observed: "the acceptance of English in its lingua franca role is consensual."

It is clear to disinterested observation that adoption of English around the world is not a result of anglophone conspiracy; learners are not, either grudgingly or unthinkingly, simply identifying with linguistic aggressors. In fact, the increasingly utilitarian acceptance of English has actually spurred activity in behalf of smaller languages: it is unsurprising to find both courses followed simultaneously.

Conspiracy and imperialism aside, there are valid fears that English will overtake other languages in more and more domains. Important voices cry out against linguistic dislocations. Ngũgĩ wa Thiong'o, the Kenyan novelist who may yet become a Nobel Prize winner, forsook English to write in his maternal Gĩkũyũ, a decision that underpins his many impassioned pleas for the linguistic and cultural "decolonizing" of the African mind. On the other hand, Chinua Achebe, an equally prominent African writer, means to use the language (English) that he has been given. Besides encouraging parallel literatures in local languages and big ones, Achebe also points to the emergence of "new Englishes," those localized variants that are more and more common around the world.

Opinion can vary about the spread of English, but it is quite unreasonable to expect that it can be meaningfully affected if the language itself is made the central target of action; this appears to be the error that many language revivalists repeatedly fall into. Languages are components of larger cultural packages and unless people take quite revolutionary steps to unpack and then repack them—which they are generally unwilling to do—then lasting linguistic changes are unlikely to occur. To hope for such changes while wishing to retain other parts of those "packages," which often include such desirable entities as modernity and mobility, is to hope for the unattainable.

The pressures that big languages exert upon smaller ones are most obvious and most severe when the latter have no official clout. For languages without a state behind them, appeals to their once-and-future speakers often rest upon pillars of cultural continuity and tradition. These are far from ignoble quantities, but they can loom less large when mundane needs are more immediate. And what about small languages fortunate enough to have their own states? Are they significantly better armed for resistance operations? The short answer is yes, but it would be a great error to think that the acquisition of official language status means that a corner of safety has been decisively turned. Irish is the only Celtic language to have its own country, but that has not made it the most dominant in its family, nor has political independence barred or, more importantly, really *wanted* to bar foreign linguistic influence at the border crossings. Other varieties (Dutch, Danish, Finnish, and Swedish, for example, to say nothing of Provençal, Catalan, Welsh, and others) are also finding that long-standing and official status at the state or regional level is no guarantee of protection.

The global expansion of English escalated considerably after World War II, although the initial formulation of the Treaty of Versailles in English rather than French was a significant watershed in international practice. Now, the great majority of the world's scholarly literature appears in English, although at least half of it is produced by authors from non-anglophone countries. Still, the increasing electronic shrinkage of the world may be good for smaller varieties. Early studies of Internet communication revealed that English had pride of place, but later ones show a growing presence of many other languages, and there is little doubt that a more multilingual Web is good for linguistic diversity.

Chapter 6
Loyalty, maintenance, shift, loss, and revival

All languages and all dialects are bearers of identity; all can have a psychological and symbolic significance that accompanies their more obvious communicative value. Speakers of big languages need hardly consider this. Minority-group members, however, rarely have the luxury of neglect here: for them, the instrumental and symbolic aspects of their language often become disengaged. This is why sociolinguistics pays closer attention to them than to "mainstream"-group members: the greater cultural and linguistic fragility of small groups tends to throw linguistic matters into sharper relief. The most obvious and therefore the most studied of such groups are ethnonational communities that have become minorities in their own country—through invasion, federation, partition. or other state-altering arrangements—or which have become small through migration.

Arguments have been made that different adaptations ought to be made for these two sorts of groups. Perhaps indigenous communities merit more official attention, greater social benefits or wider political autonomy, on the assumption that they are "autochthonous'" ("of the soil") and were "here first." Perhaps immigrant groups should expect a little less; after all, they moved and, in all but unconscionable instances, they did so voluntarily. Since there are clear linguistic aspects here, a little digression is in order, to point out that matters are less than clear-cut—as they are for the designation "minority" itself.

Is French in Canada a minority language, for example? The answer depends on the geographic perspective (provincial, regional, continental) that one adopts. And what about minorities within minorities? The aboriginal groups in Québec come to mind here, as do the Abkhazian and Ossetian enclaves within the former Soviet republic of Georgia. In many cases, groups of minority status are not particularly sensitive to the perceived plight of still smaller communities within them. Many *Québécois* nationalists who argue for the right to secede from Canada would deny that same course of action to the James Bay Cree. Numbers are also important in determining minority status, but they are not the whole story nor its most important element. Native language groups in South Africa have always vastly outnumbered speakers of English and Afrikaans, but those groups were of marginal status. It is clear that historically subaltern rank has much more to do with power than with population.

The most obvious point of comparison between indigenous and immigrant minority groups is that the former retain their residence on an ancestral home territory, something that may encourage cultural continuity, even with the loss of power and status. But there are complicating factors here, chief among which is the temporal dimension. Among the present-day Tamils of Sri Lanka, some came to the island a thousand years ago, while others moved there in the mid-nineteenth century. Are some indigenous and others not? How will we regard the apparently permanent *Gastarbeiter* ("guest workers" of the 1960s and '70s) in Europe five hundred years hence? Are the Welsh and Bretons truly indigenous in the lands they now live in? Were they not historical interlopers in some earlier age? If Canada and the United States are countries of immigrants, have some now moved to indigenous status with the passage of time? Is the

English-speaking population also an immigrant one in the eyes of aboriginal groups? And, in their turn, were not the latter also migrants via the Bering Strait?

Attachments to language become more salient when groups come into contact. The "language loyalty" that emerges is, of course, intimately intertwined with a broader group loyalty, with an identity now brought to the fore, and perhaps under perceived threat. Consequently, any communicative shift away from the ancestral variety is likely to mean discomfort and disruption, even when it is the result of "free" choice. I put the word in quotation marks because many choices that people make of their own volition are in effect Hobson's choices—that is, no real choice at all: recall Henry Ford's putative offer of a new Model T in any color, providing it was black. A better analogy, perhaps, is with *zugzwang*, the chess term for an undesirable move that nevertheless must be made. Who, after all, would move to a foreign culture and language if one were quite satisfied at home? Emigrants may not have been directly forced into those third-class or steerage quarters, but circumstances often meant that staying at home would be a fool's option.

While the presence of an original language is an obviously strong support for cultural continuity, a sense of groupness can rest upon other pillars, too (religion comes immediately to mind). The essence of that continuity, in fact, lies in the preservation over time of boundaries, of recognized group perimeters. This was the great insight of Fredrik Barth, the Norwegian social anthropologist. The continuing presence of borders is of signal importance; the cultural content that lies within them, and which gives them their permanence, can be quite mutable. Classic examples here are found in cross-generational comparisons of immigrants. The current descendants of those first Italians, Germans, and Irish to arrive in the United States look remarkably alike now; most of their cultural "markers" have altered a great deal, and very few of them speak their ancestral languages. Nor, indeed, is there any broad interest in learning them. Languages whose symbolic significance once complemented ordinary utility have lost the latter dimension, but not necessarily the former. This phenomenon also extends to indigenous groups. In an extensive attitude study undertaken in 1975, continuingly potent sentimental attachments to Irish were revealed, but these were not accompanied by much language use, nor by any widespread desire to actively promote Irish, nor yet by optimism about its future.

Those contemporary "hyphenated" Americans who are now monolingual English speakers may have forgotten the painful vernacular transitions that earlier generations had to undergo. The retention of language at a purely symbolic level is not an insignificant thing, and it may link importantly with other features of cultural life: a general interest in the past or a more specific concern with history and literature. It *might* even prove a platform for some degree of vernacular revival. It is not the same, however, as the instrumental language that gives rise to it and in whose absence more intangible aspects must ultimately fade.

Language decline

A once-popular view was that languages were almost organic, almost possessing a natural lifespan. In his Welsh-English dictionary, *The British Language in Its Lustre* (1688), Thomas Jones wrote that:

> to Languages as well as Dominions . . . there is an appointed time; they have had their infancy, foundations and beginning, their growth and increase in purity and perfection; as also in spreading, and propagation: their state of consistency; and their old age, declinings and decays.

The great nineteenth-century German linguist, Franz Bopp, also suggested that languages should be thought of as organic bodies, developing as though they had an "inner principle of life." These were metaphoric expressions even when they were written; no one believes that languages live and breathe. But organic metaphors have an appeal because, after all, languages *do* have lifespans. They are not granted by the laws of nature but by the vicissitudes of human culture. The fortunes of language are bound up with those of its users, and language decline or "death" reflects changes in the social circumstances of their speakers.

Language demise can occur without shift: a speech community dies out speaking its original variety, sometimes (but not always) in dramatic circumstances. The most common scenario, however, involves language contact and conflict: one language supplants another, and a process of shift is set in train, often proceeding over several generations. (A recent sociolinguistic argument held that language contact without conflict was impossible; the point was made by Peter Nelde, a Belgian linguist who was no doubt influenced by the continuing language difficulties in his country.) The most common pattern for immigrant languages in the United States has involved a three-generation shift: those stepping off the ship may learn very little English, particularly if they move into a neighborhood populated by earlier group arrivals (Chinatown, Little Italy, Germantown, and the like). Their children become bilingual, but *their* children are monolingual English speakers.

There is a number of historical reports of "last speakers," although these are not always entirely accurate. Dolly Pentreath died in 1777, allegedly the last native speaker of Cornish. Shanawdithit, who died in 1829, was the last speaker of Beothuk, a language isolate in Newfoundland. Ned Maddrell was the last speaker of Manx when he died in 1974. The last speaker of Oubykh (a language of the Caucasus) was Tevfik Esenç, who died in 1992. And Angela Sidney (d. 1992) and Marie Smith Jones (d. 2008) were the last fluent speakers of Tagish and Eyak, respectively (Athapascan languages of the Yukon and Alaska). There are two remaining speakers of

Ayapaneco, an indigenous Mexican language; unfortunately, Manuel Segovia and Isidro Velázquez refuse to talk to one another, even though they are neighbors in their little village in the state of Tabasco.

Few "last" speakers are monolingual, of course: they are important individual signposts of language decline as a result of group shift. Short of draconian and undesirable intervention, this is a difficult process to halt, for a simple if often disregarded reason: language shift is typically a *symptom* of contact between two unequal societies, contact in which the attractions and pressures of the stronger increasingly invade the domains of the weaker. This process is often abetted, grudging though the endorsement may be, by members of that latter group. In any event, attempts to reverse language shift generally reveal that attention to symptoms rather than causes is likely to be fruitless. One doesn't cure measles by putting bandages over the spots. And attending to the causes that underpin language shift is extremely difficult, short of revolutionary upheavals that are usually seen as impractical or unattractive.

What activists usually wish to see is a selective *linguistic* intervention in a changed or changing social fabric. Irish revivalists, or those concerned to shore up flagging varieties in North America—to cite both indigenous and immigrant settings—are typically unwilling to give up many of the socially advantageous historical developments that have occurred, developments covering everything from improved health to material prosperity, from the relaxation of traditional prejudice and intolerance to greatly enlarged possibilities of physical, social, and psychological mobility. I do not suggest that exposure to English was necessary for these desirable developments, merely that it is difficult to make a broadly compelling case, on either pragmatic or cultural grounds, for attempting to alter just a selected part of the tightly interwoven fabric of social evolution.

Language maintenance

The maintenance of a language generally rests upon the continuation of settings in which that language, and no other, is required. I have called these settings the *domains of necessity*, and they include the home, the school, and the workplace. There are many other domains, of course, but those in which participation is voluntary, sporadic, or idiosyncratic are not likely to be central to language maintenance. It is the progressive absorption of domains by a new language that charts the course of shift. The emerging patterns are rarely random: public settings are generally affected earlier than private ones, for example. That is why contemporary scholars have placed so much emphasis on the family: so long as the children learn at their mother's knee, surely the parental language will continue. In an isolated sense this is true, but it neglects the fact that even family members have to go out into the world beyond the garden gate.

There are two major and interrelated factors involved in language maintenance efforts, one tangible and one more subjective. The tangible one is that continuation of those domains of necessity just referred to. This is not an easy task. The other involves the collective *will* to stem discontinuity, to sustain linguistic vigor. Given the formidable social, economic, and cultural attractions associated with large languages and their societies, it is not surprising that active moves for language maintenance are usually the preserve of only a small number of people. There are all sorts of practical reasons why the masses cannot usually involve themselves in maintenance efforts, and although a broad goodwill often exists, it is generally a passive quantity. To galvanize social inertia has always been the most pressing issue for language activists.

It may be thought that invoking willpower is hardly appropriate when discussing groups who are under strong cultural and linguistic pressure. As an Irish scholar observed, "the lack of will to stop shrinking is an intrinsic characteristic of a shrinking language community." If small communities cannot muster sufficient will to counter external pressure, perhaps they might find themselves participating in some blame-the-victim melodrama. This is certainly to be considered. External influences, linguistic and otherwise, have often been welcomed, however, by those who see them leading to the enhancement of life chances. Beyond this, there are some further subtleties that broad-brush perspectives may not capture. While the decline of the Celtic languages has revealed familiar patterns of retreat before the advance of English, acquiescence in at least some facets of language shift (notably in educational settings) coincided with strong resistance to other manifestations of external pressure. The parents who were apparently willing enough for their children to be educated through English were at the same time quite capable of violent protest over land-management or religious matters. The suggestion, therefore, is that conscious decisions were taken, that the notion of an unnuanced surrender to overwhelming force is inaccurate. The Highland Scots, for example, increasingly came to associate English with three life-altering phenomena. Two of these were employment and prosperity; the third, emigration to the Lowlands or overseas, became recognized as the price for material advancement.

Changing fortunes have linguistic connotations. The Irish folklorist Caoimhín Ó Danachair wrote that Irish in the early nineteenth century became linked with "penury, drudgery and backwardness." Self-perceptions of Gaelic in Nova Scotia were described by Charles Dunn in almost exactly the same words: the language implied "toil, hardship and scarcity," while English was a medium of "refinement and culture." From the time of the earliest emigrations, settlers in the New World "carried with them the idea that education was coincident with a knowledge of English," as John Lorne Campbell observed. I am making no judgment here about the accuracy or the desirability of such attitudes but only point out that perceptions of languages, and the desires and actions that rest upon them, are based on comparative assessments. As resistance in other quarters indicates, there is some evidence for a reasoned discrimination here, even in subject populations.

Even if people have seemed less likely to go to the barricades for language than for other things, there are nonetheless examples of linguistic willpower. After enduring long years of sociopolitical and religious paternalism, the francophone population in Québec experienced a *révolution tranquille*, transformed and modernized itself, and assumed the provincial mastery that its inherent strength had always promised. An important corollary of the transformation was linguistic engineering on behalf of a French language considered to be at risk. Conscious effort occurs at the individual level, too: parents are often determined to bring their children up in quite specific linguistic ways. And, if one family can make certain choices, others might follow. Consider the far-reaching effects of Eliezer Ben-Yehuda's creation, in the 1880s, of the first Hebrew-speaking home in what was to become Israel; his son, born in 1882, was the first maternally Hebrew-speaking child in the modern era.

Language nationalists, activists, and enthusiasts of all stripes also testify to the importance of will, to the strength of commitments and often-dashed hopes. To stay with the Celtic world, consider the Cornish and Manx revivalists. Consider those native anglophones who move to the *Gaeltachtaí* (the Irish-speaking areas) of Ireland and Scotland, or who help establish Irish and Gaelic schools in Dublin, Edinburgh, and Glasgow. Consider those who carry the banners for Gaelic in Nova Scotia, making sure that the road signs that once read only "Antigonish County" now also show *Siorramachd Antagonais*. The other side of this coin, the one that often lends poignancy to language activism, is the will of those who choose *not* to move to minority-speaking enclaves, or to bring up their children in some endangered medium, or to otherwise encourage a "small" language.

The importance of linguistic and cultural will and its ramifications can hardly be denied, and it is a quantity that rests, ultimately,

5. The depiction on this 1959 stamp of Eliezer Ben-Yehuda, revivalist of the Hebrew language, is an indication of the importance of a common language in what would become Israel.

upon perception and attitude. As Ernest Renan observed more than a century ago, "une nation est une âme, un principe spirituel," in which the single most important factor is the group will. In fact, he contrasted this explicitly with language: "il y a dans l'homme quelque chose de supérieur à la langue; c'est la volonté." (A nation, that is to say, is a spiritual entity that rests more upon will than upon a particular language.)

Language maintenance is usually a parlous enterprise because by the time a small variety is seen to stand in need of it, the precipitating social pressures have often assumed large proportions. This is why maintenance and outright revival can generally be considered under the same rubric. (The famous case of the Hebrew revival in Israel stands somewhat apart, of course, although the linguistic and social factors there were not unique in themselves.) Just as contemporary linguists disdain prescriptivism—often forgetting that *any* type of language planning necessarily means prescriptivism—so most (but not all) have traditionally seen a "naturalness" to language decline and shift that precludes any useful intervention, even if it were thought broadly desirable. Joshua Fishman (see chap. 5) has regretted mother-tongue loss among groups "who have not capitulated to the massive blandishments of Western materialism, who experience life and nature in deeply poetic and collectively meaningful ways"; he argues that trying to reverse language shift is a holy quest. Attempting to combine scholarship and advocacy or, at least, attending to each of them under the same disciplinary rubric may be an unwise and unpropitious course.

A final note

Maintenance and revival efforts are usually best understood as reflections of the wish to shore up an important constituent of group identity. Since a stand-alone monolingualism is increasingly less likely and less desired in small cultural contexts, treatments of these efforts are essentially discussions about the best arrangement of multilingual and multicultural adaptations, either within or across state borders. At least at their deeper levels, such discussions are philosophical debates about social life writ large. It is always salutary to bear this in mind when considering particular manifestations of pluralism, linguistic or otherwise.

Chapter 7
Multilingualism

Accommodations are frequently desirable or necessary in multilingual or multidialectal settings—and some occur at finer-grained levels, too. Important here are the related concepts of "register" (which refers to contextual or functional variants: the language of law, for instance, or medical language) and "style" (referring to adjustments of formality, which can be anchored at one end by the language of intimacy and, at the other, by language that is frozen in print). Where register becomes unnecessarily impenetrable, overly specialized, or downright nonsensical, it may be deemed "jargon." Where it draws heavily upon nonstandard and often ephemeral usage, "slang" may be a more appropriate term.

Convergence with, or divergence from, conversational partners is common. Manipulation of accent and dialect features may occur, as well as alterations in speech rate and intensity, changes of subject, reworking of message content, and so on. Phatic communication, the virtually information-less "small talk" that nevertheless acts as a sort of social grooming, reflects adaptation. Paralinguistic features like tone and pitch, hesitation and pausing also contribute to the framing and interpretation of messages. And nonverbal accompaniments, including gestures, changes of physical distance, posture and orientation, actual contact (haptics), gaze and facial expressions, are also part of the accommodative package. Research has shown, in fact, that

Box E
From George Eliot's *Middlemarch* (1871–72). Here, the irresponsible Fred Vincy is discussing language with his sister, Rosamond:

Fred: ". . . all choice of words is slang. It marks a class."

Rosamond: "There is correct English: that is not slang."

Fred: "I beg your pardon: correct English is the slang of prigs who write history and essays. And the strongest slang of all is the slang of poets."

Fred does not understand slang in the contemporary sense, but the essence of his argument is surely a very modern one.

listeners who perceive discrepancies between verbal and nonverbal messages are more likely to believe the latter.

Bilingualism and multilingualism

The most immediately noticeable adaptations, of course, involve learning and using other languages and dialects. In many settings, bilingual accommodation seems the obvious avenue: one language for home and family, a variety that reinforces intimacy and helps to maintain historical continuity; another for the world beyond one's gate, a language of necessity.

While bilingual or multilingual capabilities can be approached at both the individual and the social level, the two are not always neatly connected. A region whose population is almost entirely multilingual may nevertheless officially recognize only one or two varieties. Many African countries, for example, have two official languages, usually a strong indigenous variety and an important European one, for highly heterogeneous and multilingual populations. On the other hand, many of the citizens of an officially bilingual or multilingual state may be monolingual. Beyond the province of Québec—in which French is the only official variety, but where many urban-dwellers are bilingual—Canada is overwhelmingly English-only, despite its official and much-vaunted federal bilingualism. (I am leaving aside here the sizable "allophone" population which, in Canada, means non-English, non-French, and non-aboriginal-language speakers: essentially, newer immigrants.) It is unlike those African populations that maintain their many languages over time, for two main reasons: first, because it is an immigrant population with every expectation of language accommodations; second, because while the "heritage" varieties brought from overseas may last for a generation or so, the groups move rather steadily toward the English "mainstream." Bilingualism is often, in fact, an impermanent way station on the road to a new monolingualism.

Where bilingualism remains more permanent, usually involving continuingly different social functions and domains of use for each language, the term "diglossia" is often used—even though, as the Greek version of the Latin "bilingualism," it doesn't logically cover any different ground. The connotation, nevertheless, is of a long-term phenomenon. Still, even stability is relative. The French-English diglossia that prevailed in England after the Norman Conquest eventually broke down.

Why should bilingualism (or multilingualism) be of particular sociolinguistic interest? It is an ability possessed by the majority of human beings—most of them relatively uneducated, many of them illiterate—which, in appropriate circumstances, can be acquired quite easily, even by the young. Why should a second or subsequent language warrant more than an extending footnote to the broader linguistic inquiry? Second-language acquisition cannot in principle be a precise replica of mother-tongue learning, simply because it *is* second: Heraclitus told us that you can't step into the same river twice. There is, therefore, a large technical literature on bilingualism. Since most of it falls under the rubric of psycholinguistics rather than sociolinguistics, however, I omit it here, suggesting only that a main vein of interest lies under the heading of identity.

Speaking a particular language means belonging to a particular speech community; speaking two or more may imply some sort of dual citizenship. Since language is a central personality trait, one possibility is that bilinguals have an identity woven out of more than one linguistic thread. Another is that personalities themselves may be dual. Much of interest rests upon the degree to which bilinguals possess either two (theoretically) separate systems of language, from each of which they can draw as circumstances warrant, or some more intertwined linguistic capacity. Compelling data are hard to come by here.

Linguistic adaptation to circumstances was of particular interest to Edward Sapir and his pupil Benjamin Lee Whorf. The linguistic hypothesis named after them captured the very old view that different languages carve up reality in different ways. In its strongest form, the argument is that your language determines the way you see and think about the world. A tight connection here would powerfully underpin the position held by all those who believe in an inviolable equation between a particular language and the group identity of its speakers. However, this "strong Whorfianism" is not generally accepted. The greatest counterarguments are that while languages obviously differ in important ways, we can translate among them, and that speakers of one variety whose circumstances change can learn another.

In its "weaker" form, Whorfianism makes a great deal of sense: language can *influence* our *habitual* ways of thinking. If we find that the Inuit talk and think about snow in a much more fine-grained and engrossing way than do Italians, we should simply understand that important features of their physical, social, and psychological environments are quite different. A desert community whose color vocabulary was traditionally nuanced in reds and browns but limited in greens would doubtless expand appropriately after the group struck oil and moved to Ireland. Environments of all kinds can be expected to "set" perceptions in particular ways, and every instance reinforces the particular linguistic parameters that highlight it. But none of this implies the development of some unalterable cognitive rigidity.

Incidentally, the notion that the Inuit have many different words— suggestions have ranged as high as four hundred—to refer to various types and conditions of what English speakers simply term "snow" is incorrect. In an amusing and enlightening book, Geoffrey Pullum has shown that they do not have distinct words for "snow on the ground," "fallen snow," "slushy snow," "snow drift," and all the rest. Pointing out that the phenomenon would be trivial even if true, Pullum cited authoritative sources that show only two relevant lexical roots: *ganik* (referring to snow in the air) and *aput* (snow on the ground). Many words can then be derived from these, just as "snow" in English can produce "snowfall," "snowflake," and "snowball."

In any event, what is the significance of a bilingualism that links an individual to more than one language community? Sometimes it is quite minor: the purely instrumental fluencies needed to conduct simple business transactions do not represent much of a psychological excursion from one's linguistic base camp. Still, there are many bilinguals whose competence is more deep seated and whose abilities go beyond spartan instrumentality. Some have a (real or alleged) kinship attachment to each group; others may have acquired second and subsequent linguistic citizenships in more formal ways. Some have written about their own experiences, and a few have speculated on the bilingualism condition more generally: I am thinking here of Steiner, Conrad, Nabokov, Kundera, Stoppard, and the others whose literary skills have encouraged meaningful reflection. We can learn from them, but they are atypical. Most bilinguals are less introspective, less articulate, more "ordinary." We need more sociolinguistic reports from those quarters.

Everyone is bilingual. At least, there is no adult who does not know at least a few foreign words and phrases: for anglophones, these include such terms as *c'est la vie* or *gracias* or *guten Tag* or *tovarisch*. While few would consider such limited competence as bilingualism, it is reasonable to ask at what point fluencies become sufficient to merit the term. How, in other words, should bilingualism be defined and measured? Earlier approaches tended to be more restrictive than later ones. In 1933 Leonard Bloomfield argued that bilingualism meant the addition of a perfectly learned second variety to one's first and undiminished language. Twenty years later Einar Haugen suggested that the ability to produce complete utterances in the second language was a sufficient criterion. But most modern treatments agree that specific contexts and specific purposes should be considered.

The question of degree, of where bilingualism really "starts," is complicated by the several relevant dimensions of ability: listening, speaking, reading, and writing. One could be a reasonably good "receptive" (or "passive") bilingual but not a very good "productive" (or "active") one. As well, facility across the levels of vocabulary, grammar, and pronunciation may vary a great deal. Should some equivalence across these dimensions be sought, or might sufficient strength in one compensate for weakness in another? A rough sense of bilingual proficiency can usually be arrived at, of course, but it may not be sufficient for comparing bilingualism across individuals, or for relating language abilities to other personality characteristics.

There are all sorts of tests available to measure bilingualism: some involve self-report, others use interviews, or measures of relative dominance and linguistic flexibility. Reaction times to information presented in two (or more, of course) languages may be useful in determining relative strengths, vocabulary tests can be used, pronunciations can be recorded and assessed, and so on. There are many hazards in applying and interpreting such tests, because they can be affected by a host of factors: attitude, age, gender, intelligence, memory, linguistic distance between the languages, and context of testing. Furthermore, even if it were possible to make accurate assessments, problems of appropriate labeling would remain: after all, one would hardly expect people to fall neatly into a small number of ability compartments. Two things are clear, though: there are very few truly "balanced bilinguals," individuals whose skills are equivalent across their languages; relatedly, the vast majority of those to whom the term "bilingual" can be reasonably applied show marked dominance for one of their languages.

It has sometimes been thought that proficiency in one language may mean diminished ability in another, but there is no evidence for such a view of mental capacity. Even if some "finite-container" model were to be accepted, all that is known of intellectual structures and functions suggests that there is no likelihood of exceeding neural limits. Sherlock Holmes justified his ignorance of many things by telling Watson that the brain was like an attic, that one should fill it wisely according to one's needs, and that "it is a mistake to think that that little room has elastic walls and can distend to any extent." Holmes could have remedied his ignorance of literature and astronomy, however, without displacing his knowledge of poisons or the many varieties of cigarette ash.

There have always been people with extraordinary linguistic fluencies, and they seem not to have paid any sort of cognitive price. Richard Francis Burton, the Victorian soldier-explorer, traveled widely in India, Arabia, and North and South America. He was competent or better in more than two dozen languages. Or consider James Murray: destined to be the first editor of the *Oxford English Dictionary*, he applied in 1866 for a post in the British Library, outlining his very impressive linguistic credentials. Here is part of his letter of application:

I possess a general acquaintance with the languages and literature of the Aryan and Syro-Arabic classes . . . with several [languages] I have a more intimate acquaintance, as with the Romance tongues, Italian, French, Catalan, Spanish, Latin and in a less degree Portuguese, Vaudois, Provençal and various dialects. In the Teutonic branch I am tolerably familiar with Dutch . . . Flemish, German, Danish. In Anglo-Saxon and Moeso-Gothic my studies have been much closer . . . I know a little of the Celtic, and am at present engaged with the Sclavonic [sic], having obtained a useful knowledge of Russian. In the Persian, Achaemenian Cuneiform and Sanscrit branches, I know for the purposes of Comparative Philology. I have sufficient knowledge of Hebrew and Syriac to read at sight the OT [Old Testament] . . . to a less degree I know Aramaic Arabic, Coptic and Phenician [sic].

Remarkable though Murray and Burton were, particularly by contemporary anglophone standards, such multiplication of capabilities is not confined to exceptional cases. Paulin Djité, a friend and colleague of mine, grew up in Côte d'Ivoire speaking French and Wè at home, and Yoruba, Baoulé, and Dyula with playmates and others. His education was through French, English, and Spanish. As an adolescent, he added Attié, Gouro, Koulango, Dida, and Bété to his linguistic repertoire, along with a more passive knowledge of Ewe and other varieties. His language skills are formidable, but as he himself has pointed out, many educated Africans have followed similar linguistic paths.

The general point is simple: bilingualism is not risky. An important corollary is that bringing children up bilingually, enrolling them in bilingual-education programs, or placing them in appropriately constructed school "immersion" environments, is not risky either. Where negative consequences of bilingualism have been observed, language itself is rarely to blame; some constellation of social, personal, or cultural factors is typically the culprit. Beyond its effects on school children, bilingualism has also been seen as socially risky in some quarters. In the United States, some have felt

6. Sir James Murray, first editor of the *Oxford English Dictionary*, is seen here in his "scriptorium" (a room for writing), which he had had built in his garden in Oxford.

that bilingual education for Spanish-speaking children may delay their acquisition of English and thus interfere with full integration. The evidence, in fact, suggests otherwise. It seems clear that worries about social divisiveness are often underpinned by fears of some creeping Hispanicization, and are sometimes fueled by darker motives altogether.

Most scholars point to the advantages of bilingual competence acquired in childhood and, in some accounts, younger brains are seen to be more "plastic" and "flexible" than older ones. There is something to this—particularly, perhaps, where accurate accent acquisition is involved—but older learners have learning experience that is lacking in small children and, providing the motivation is sufficient, they often prove to be better learners. If the maturity and articulated necessity of the older were combined with the impressionability, imitativeness, spontaneity, and unselfconsciousness of the younger, rapid and proficient bilingual acquisition could be predicted.

Theories of second-language learning, like those of mother-tongue acquisition, endorse a cognitive sequence in which rules are formulated and tested. The major difference, perhaps, lies in the context. That is, all normal children will have learned their first language quite well by an early age; learning second and subsequent ones, however, is clearly a less "automatic" process and more one in which social context is paramount. Contemporary anglophone laments about the difficulty of learning another language reveal more about the current state of global realities than they do about inherent disadvantage. For those many millions who do become bi- or multilingual, mundane necessity is the great motivator and the great determiner of how far language competence develops.

It is one thing to say that all normal people have the basic capacity to expand their linguistic repertoires and that doing so exacts no intellectual penalties. But what of the notion that bilingualism can *increase* intellectual scope? There is a long historical tradition that one's personality somehow expands with increased language fluencies, held particularly among the social elite for whom an additional language or two was always an integral part of civilized life. In the sixteenth century, Charles V (again) suggested that *quot linguas calles, tot homines vales*: one becomes as many people as languages known. There is some minority opinion on the matter, though. In the seventeenth century, for instance, John Milton and Samuel Butler argued that expanded repertoires do not, in themselves, imply intellectual breadth. Milton said that multiple language fluencies alone were no substitute for underlying knowledge; Butler wrote that "the more languages a man can speak, his talent has but sprung the greater leak."

In the modern era, scholarly investigation once tended to associate bilingualism with lowered intelligence. Some of this work was reinforced or prompted by racist reactions to the early twentieth-century flood of immigrants to America. As part of the burgeoning intelligence-testing movement of the time, in which assessments were constructed to screen uneducated, nonwhite, and non-northern-European arrivals, it was often found that "feeble-mindedness" among immigrants (or hopefuls) was correlated with poor knowledge of English. A widely cited study by Florence Goodenough concluded that "the use of a foreign language in the home is one of the chief factors in producing mental retardation." Amazing, perhaps, but understandable at a time when social fears and prejudices underpinned not only racism but also programs of eugenics and involuntary sterilization supported by many prominent scholars and statesmen.

The excesses of this era became increasingly apparent, and so too did more nuanced difficulties. Almost all the early work attempting to relate bilingualism to intelligence was flawed by inadequate experimental controls. A representative study found no significant intelligence difference between urban monolingual and bilingual children, but a substantial one among rural children:

it had neglected to take into account marked socioeconomic variations among their parents. In all such work, too, there are problems of reasonable inference. If a negative correlation were to be found between intelligence and bilingual ability, which has caused which? There might be other, unmeasured factors that influence both, and thus create the observed relationship. The old maxim applies: correlation need not imply causation. As more careful studies paid closer attention to nonlinguistic factors, that relationship essentially evaporated.

What some have seen as a turning point came in the early 1960s, when findings showing a *positive* relationship between intelligence and bilingualism began to appear. Studies in Montreal found that children bilingual in French and English outperformed their monolingual counterparts on both verbal and nonverbal intelligence tests, leading Robert Gardner and Wallace Lambert to conclude that the former possessed "mental flexibility, a superiority in concept formation, and a more diversified set of mental abilities." They also acknowledged the correlational problem: "it is not possible to state from the present study whether the more intelligent child became bilingual or whether bilingualism aided his [*sic*] intellectual development." The most recent work, also undertaken by Canadian researchers, has nevertheless suggested that bilingualism is associated with improved cognitive functioning. It has also argued that the larger "cognitive reserves" of bilinguals may ameliorate the symptoms of Alzheimer's disease; unsurprisingly, this has attracted considerable media attention. The researchers acknowledge some limitations and note that the performance of bilinguals is not invariably better than that of their monolingual counterparts.

Overall, it seems fair to say that strong conclusions about bilingualism and cognition are not warranted. The enlargement of the linguistic repertoire is, in itself, unlikely to lead to significantly increased cognitive and intellectual skills. It is obviously, however, a highly desirable personal expansion.

Beyond bilingualism

Despite the many nuances that are available to all normal speakers, monoglot or polyglot, efficient communication often requires further action, and this falls into two categories. The first involves lingua francas. Although there were no doubt earlier examples, the classic lingua franca (that is to say, the "language of the Franks") was a medium for trade and commerce dating from the time of the Crusaders' struggles in the eastern Mediterranean. It drew upon several languages, including Provençal, French, and Italian, with the last being the dominant element. Turkish, Greek, and Arabic also contributed, and the word "Frank" clearly suggests Eastern influence: it is related to *feringhi*, an Arabic word denoting any European (or, sometimes, any Christian). Early uses of the term typically refer to some sort of "mixed language," and it appears for the first time in English in the late seventeenth century: a lingua franca, one of John Dryden's characters says, is a compound of all tongues. The meaning then generalized to signify any "contact" medium, and by the end of the nineteenth century, the term had expanded to include instances where a single language provided the necessary bridging. Although the earlier connotation of a mixture of varieties was not entirely lost, this last sense grew, and today the most common lingua francas are the big world languages.

There are many historical examples of existing languages becoming important lingua francas—not because of any intrinsic qualities setting them above other varieties but because of the power and prestige of their speakers, native or otherwise. Greek and Latin are the classical examples, but French, Italian, Arabic, Hindi, and other languages have all played bridging roles.

Pidgins and creoles have also acted as "link languages," often between European traders and the local people with whom they dealt. In his *Voyage to China*, published in 1850, Julius Berncastle suggested that "pidgin" was a Chinese mispronunciation of

Box F
The term "lingua franca," as found in John Dryden's
play *The Kind Keeper, or, Mr. Limberham* (1680)

Woodall: *Seignior, io non canno takare ten guinneo possibilmentè; 'tis to my losso.*

Limberham: That is, Pug, he cannot possibly take ten guineas, 'tis to his loss: Now I understand him; this is almost English.

Mrs Tricksy: English! away, you fop: 'tis a kind of *lingua Franca*, as I have heard the merchants call it; a certain compound language, made up of all tongues, that passes through the Levant.

Limberham: This *lingua*, what you call it, is the most rarest language! I understand it as well as if it were English; you shall see me answer him: *Seignioro, stay a littlo, and consider wello, ten guinnio is monyo, a very considerablo summo*.

"business," but this is a disputed etymology. The important point is that pidgin varieties employ only those restricted vocabularies and grammars needed for simple and practical communication. Little nuance is required. (Pidgins exemplify a much more general linguistic tendency, in fact: the development of fluencies up to, but not beyond, the requirements of day-to-day use.) Pidgins are often quite ephemeral, but in situations in which contacts are prolonged, they may have some longevity.

In Papua New Guinea, Tok Pisin (i.e., "talk pidgin") is spoken by several million people and has achieved official recognition. From Luke 15:31, in the New Testament (*Nupela Testamen*), comes "I tokim em, i spik, 'Pikinini, oltaim oltaim yumi tupela i save stap wantaim. Na olgeta samting bilong mi em bilong yu.'" This is Tok Pisin for "he said unto him, 'Son, thou art ever with me, and all that I have is thine'" (KJV). In fact, Tok Pisin has now become the mother tongue for some people, which means it has become an "expanded pidgin" or, indeed, a *creole*.

Definitions of "creole" vary considerably, but they all begin with people rather than language: a person of European ancestry—of French or Spanish background in Louisiana, the Caribbean, or Latin America, for example; or a person of mixed white European and black heritage; or, indeed, Africans born in non-African colonies. In its traditional linguistic sense, a creole emerges when children born in pidgin-speaking communities begin to develop (or "creolize") their linguistic inheritance. Nobody's mother tongue becomes somebody's mother tongue in a process by which the emerging variety becomes richer and more expressive than its parent. Scholars have also suggested, however, that creole varieties may arise "abruptly," from group contact without any preceding pidgin stage. A national language of Sierra Leone is Krio (i.e., Creole); it is spoken by the vast majority of the country's six million inhabitants. And now, in combination with other languages, Krio spawns further pidgin varieties: a nice example of the ever-dynamic nature of language.

A final type of lingua franca is the "artificial" or constructed language, of which there have been a great many over the centuries. The most well known and by far the most successful is Esperanto, published by Ludwig Zamenhof in 1887. It has between one hundred thousand and two million speakers today, a range that reveals the inadequacy of current estimates. As well, there are several hundred children for whom Esperanto is the mother tongue. Zamenhof, like other makers and supporters of constructed language, hoped that Esperanto would provide more than a universal second language; it might also contribute to a desirable "transnational identity," one that would counter the violent excesses of nationalism.

The idea of a neutral auxiliary language has seemed appealing to many people. Such a variety does not privilege any particular national group, it has no unpleasant historical baggage, it is constructed so as to be easily learned, and it supplements rather than replaces "natural" mother tongues. But no Esperanto-like production has succeeded in any but the most restricted and self-conscious settings. Some critics have bluntly dismissed constructed-language apologists as cranks, faddists, and "language maniacs." Others, while not always wholly unsympathetic, have pointed to flaws. A historically persistent view—espoused by commentators as various as Bertrand Russell, George Bernard Shaw, H. L. Mencken, George Steiner, and J. R. R. Tolkien—is that languages simply do not arrive on the scene in such precipitate fashion. They emerge, rather, over long periods of time, carrying with them histories, literatures, myths, and traditions. Mencken thus complained that "universal" languages lack the "juices of life," and Steiner wrote that they were without any "natural semantics of remembrance."

Collaborating with Charles Ogden, Ivor Richards presented "Basic English" in 1930: like Esperanto, it was intended as an international auxiliary language. Although this simplified variety attracted George Orwell for a time, he soon became disenchanted with the whole idea—although Basic English was the foundation for the "Newspeak" of his *1984*. Nellie Limouzin, an aunt of Orwell's, lived in Paris with the noted Esperantist Eugene Adam. Something of a language fanatic, Adam engaged in endless debate, which may have prompted Orwell's observation that, "for sheer dirtiness of fighting, the feud between the inventors of various of the international languages would take a lot of beating." Orwell's point is not without foundation, but Richards himself made a more general one: there has always been insufficient incentive for significant numbers of people to learn a constructed language. There is indeed a great obstacle here, perhaps now a fatal one in a modern world so thoroughly penetrated by English. An invented lingua franca like Esperanto might be more appealing if it possessed a large international body of speakers. Since it does not, however, potential learners may reasonably ask themselves why they should take the plunge. And yet, without more people learning the language, that large international speech community will never arrive. The difficulty here is a sort of Catch-22.

Although not an enthusiast myself, I find it regrettable that so few scholars have paid any substantial attention to constructed languages. They may be peripheral sociolinguistic phenomena, but they are historically long-standing ones. Apart from the language aspects per se, there are also psychological and sociological points of interest here. What are the impulses and motivations of language inventors and learners? How do the former go about their task: do they draw upon any linguistic scholarship? What sort of people are the learners? These and other questions have been neglected by an academy that has generally prejudged or seen as taboo the whole area, even though (for Esperanto, at least) there are "facts, texts, and living subjects readily available."

Beyond the lingua franca, the other great communication bridge is translation. Apart from the most elementary word-for-word exercises—rarely useful, as the Roman statesman Cicero pointed out when advising against translating *verbum pro verbo*—every act of translation involves interpretation and judgement. This means that translation happens within as well as across languages. Even the simplest of conversations between speakers of the same language can require the oral equivalent of "reading between the lines," and it is only through a constant process of translation (and periodic retranslation) that we maintain links with our own literature and our own culture.

Judgment and interpretation must be exercised carefully, and most translators respect the general admonition of John Dryden who, when translating Virgil, reported that he "thought fit to steer betwixt the two extremes of paraphrase and literal translation; to keep as near my author as I could without losing all his graces." The idea, as Dryden went on to say, was to try and make the poet "speak such English as he would himself have spoken, if he had been born in England, and in this present age." Three centuries later, the point was generalized by the classicist Émile Rieu as "the law of equivalent effect."

It is interesting to consider that the greatest threats to accurate translation, to the achievement of "equivalent effect" across time and culture, appear at opposite ends of the literary continuum. At one pole there is slang, swearing, and ephemeral idiom. When Leonard Tancock was translating the "naturalist" works of Zola into English, he pointed out that the author's use of "more or less blasphemous variations and elaborations on the *Nom de dieu!* theme" would hardly work for mid-twentieth-century English readers. Parallels had to be found, current English words and phrases of similar tenor and impact. At the other pole are poetic, dramatic, or philosophical productions rich in metaphor and allusion, or full of dense, abstract reasoning. Shakespeare presents more difficulties than Agatha Christie. (Even a writer as prosaic as Christie can create problems for translators. The late Czech-Canadian writer Josef Škvorecký noted the difficulty in turning Hercule Poirot's very "frenchified" English into something that would "work" in Czech translation.)

Accurate translation may be difficult, but its linguistic benefits are clear and continuing. They may, however, be offset by psychological disadvantages. The translator has entry to (at least) two language communities, and may be able to transport intimate information from one to the other. Successful translation, George Steiner remarked, has a touch of treason: "hoarded dreams, patents of life are being taken across the frontier." Proverbial expressions in several languages support him. To cite only two, Italian (*traduttori, traditori*) and Hungarian (*fordítás, ferdítés*) equate translation with treachery or distortion.

Chapter 8
Name, sex, and religion

It may be indelicate in modern society to ask about someone's income or political inclinations or family ancestry, but inquiring about religion has *always* called for tact and has sometimes been dangerous for those asking or replying. Similarly, conversations about sexual preferences and practices have typically been either guarded or avoided, and circumspect description of sex and gender remains the norm in polite and scholarly usage. Names and naming can also carry important emotional baggage and may prove very contentious. Little wonder, then, that religious, sexual, and onomastic matters occupy important, if sometimes rather neglected, niches within sociolinguistics. Ending this book with a discussion of these topics emphasizes that they merit fuller formal investigation. They have always been of very broad general interest.

Language and religion

Formal sociolinguistic interest in the relationship between language and religion has been much slighter than might be imagined, despite the many points of connection between the two. Among the most important of these points are language and religion as common and sometimes complementary markers of groupness, the language *of* religion, and the work of missionaries. The spread of religion, for instance, has generally had linguistic accompaniments. With the spectacular expansion of Islam in the seventh and eighth centuries, Arabic became a world language. With the fourth-century conversion of the Emperor Constantine, Latin became the lingua franca of Christianity and the old principle of *cuius regio, eius religio* (the religion of the ruler is the religion of his domains) was strongly reinforced. In the Holy Roman Empire of the sixteenth century, the principle was reaffirmed in the interests of international harmony.

Within states, too, religion and language have often been seen to march together. In revolutionary France, fewer than half the citizens were actually French-speaking, and many regional varieties were seen by the new political masters as mediums of religious fanaticism: superstition, it was said, spoke Breton; fanaticism spoke Basque. In nineteenth-century Russia, "polonization" in Lithuania was associated with Catholicism, a threat to the official Orthodox church. At about the same time, anti-French sentiment in Flanders had a strongly religious tone, and for some ultramontane Catholics language activism was but an aspect of larger religious motivations.

The Buddhist Sutras, the Hindu Vedas, the Christian Bible, the Holy Qur'an and the Hadith, the Torah and the Talmud, and many other religious works are all sacred in and of themselves, to varying degrees. Some, for instance, are not to be translated at all, while particular versions of others (the King James Bible, for example) have achieved iconic status. Even more centrally, the holiness of the "word" can reflect a sacred linkage between words and things and can, indeed, imply creation itself. The idea predates both the Christian era and the Greek Golden Age. Some time during the twenty-fifth Egyptian dynasty (i.e., ca. 750–650 BCE), an already existing theological discussion was inscribed on a stone, now in the British Museum. This "Memphite Theology" recounts how the god Ptah, having first *thought* the world, went on to create it by saying the name of all its elements. Thus, in the Egyptian mythology, as in later ones, names and things coincided, the former perfectly capturing the essence of the latter.

In the Christian tradition there is from earliest times this mystical association of the "word" (*logos*, the Greek λόγος)—with its many related meanings of word, thought, pervading principle, reason, and logic—with the all-pervasive and divine spirit. This is written at the opening of the Gospel of John in the most forthright way: "In the beginning was the Word, and the Word was with God, and the Word was God." Christ *is* the *logos*, and the "word" in biblical usage also generally implies Christian belief. Genesis 1:3 describes God creating light by *saying* "let there be light," and the holy connection here has never been broken. God commanded things into existence: *opera dei sunt verba eius* (his works are his words). It follows that any tampering with the "word" is of the utmost gravity.

There are clear demonstrations that translation can be blasphemous. He who has "been in Christ" must not (or, perhaps, cannot) repeat the *arcana verba* in mortal words (2 Cor. 12:4). And Jewish writings from the first century record the belief that the translation of the holy law into Greek led to three days of darkness. There are groups who believe that the name of God is never to be uttered, others who reserve this honor for some priestly caste, and still others who argue that *no* language at all is adequate for religious purposes. Some, like the Quakers, prefer silent worship, for only then may God's "still, small voice" (1 Kings 19:12) be heard.

From the general sense of the sacred status of language, there quickly arose more assertions about specific languages. These were based upon speculations about the language of Eden. Genesis 2:19 describes how God formed all the birds and beasts, "and brought them unto Adam to see what he would call them: and whatsoever Adam called every living creature, that was the name thereof" (KJV). This naming took place in the original, ideal, and God-given language: unlike all natural varieties since, there was thus a mystical but perfect correspondence between words and the things that they named. What *was* this first, divine language that God implanted in the first man? And how is this relevant in our discussions here?

The question of the first language was of the first importance because those who speak that language, or whose ancestors did, might claim a special and intimate relationship with divinity. Early Jewish literature unsurprisingly described Hebrew as the first language, and the view was also supported by virtually all the Greek, Latin, and (later) Byzantine patriarchs, and by the Christian community generally. Aramaic was also proposed as the original *lingua humana*, too, as was Arabic in some quarters. Well into the seventeenth and eighteenth centuries, scholars were asking related questions: Did the language of Adam survive in some form or other? Was it contemporary Hebrew? Was it the apparently nonsensical utterings, the *glossolalia*, the "speaking in tongues" of Pentecost?

Many understood, of course, that even if Hebrew were the original language, its contemporary varieties had clearly lost that essential character that allowed a perfect fit between words and things. In the mid-seventeenth century, Thomas Hobbes pointed out that, while "the first author of Speech was *God* himself, that instructed *Adam* how to name such creatures as he presented to his sight," the scriptural record "goeth no further in this matter." Besides, Hobbes added, whatever *may* have been the situation in the Garden of Eden, all of Adam's linguistic invention was "lost at the tower of *Babel*, when by the hand of God, every man was stricken for his rebellion, with an oblivion of his former language."

Suggestions for the first language included Danish, Swedish, Polish, Basque, Hungarian, German, Chinese, and all the Celtic varieties. Multiple-language scenarios were also developed. In one (French) view, God spoke Spanish to Adam, the Devil spoke Italian, and Adam and Eve subsequently apologized to God—in

French, *bien sur*. Some Persian scholars felt that Adam and Eve spoke their language, that the snake spoke Arabic, and that the angel Gabriel spoke Turkish. Such bizarre conjectures were derided as soon as they were made, and by the late seventeenth century it had become clear that the urges of identity politics and aspirations fueled the many ludicrous outbursts of special pleading. Since Latin was on the wane at this time, and since the "vulgar" tongues were coming into their own as national mediums, it is unsurprising to find competitive arguments made on their behalf. The idea that a particular language might have some claim superior to all others resonated in even the most scholarly of hearts. Leibniz joined in the ridicule, saying that if the Turks and Tartars became as learned as Europeans, they would argue that *their* languages were the mother tongues of all—but he still retained a fondness for the idea of divine "Celto-Scythian" roots that would include German.

The great nineteenth-century German philologist Max Müller pointed out that all these fruitless speculations retarded the progress of linguistic science. For example, the strong advocacy of Hebrew as the language of Eden meant that, when scholars began to seriously consider linguistic classification and language families, they devoted much time trying to show how Hebrew had produced so many offspring. "It is astonishing," Müller wrote, "what an amount of real learning and ingenuity was wasted on this question during the seventeenth and eighteenth centuries."

Most of the efforts to investigate the language of Eden, or to stake a claim for one modern variety or another as the primary descendant of that sacred variety, now seem very odd indeed. They remain of social-psychological value because, like most inquiries into the social life of language, they were really about group distinctiveness. Since they occurred at a time when biblical affiliations and divisions were of the utmost significance, the tight intertwining of linguistic and religious elements seems very natural indeed. This intertwining is still extremely powerful in many parts of the world.

Not all of them are far away, either: there are many millions of North American evangelical Christians, for instance, who continue to believe that the Bible is the *literal* word of God, for whom the ancient connotations of the *logos* still hold good.

At another level entirely, recall the Israeli context, in which the need for a common language coincided with an existing *langue intime*, one with quintessentially religious connotations. The particularity of the Israeli Hebrew "case" is that the religious factor was central, and in two ways. First, during the long period when the language almost ceased to exist as a daily vernacular, religion provided a sheltering home for it. Second, the development and maintenance of a state built upon a specific religious base brought that sheltered language back into wide mundane use.

There are other modern instances of the close connections among language, religion, and identity that are as interesting, if not always as dramatic, as those involving Hebrew. Some show how a strong connection between language and religion can both reinforce and weaken the former. If, for instance, religion is a central pillar in the culture of a group whose language is at risk, it makes sense to exploit its strength and to suggest that faith is uniquely expressible through the threatened tongue. In nineteenth-century Nova Scotia, Gaelic was equated with wisdom, honor, and righteousness, for it was "a powerful, spiritual language." Similarly, in 1916 Robert Fullerton described Irish as "the casket which encloses the highest and purest religion"—it was the "instrument and expression of a purely Catholic culture." At the same time, English could be condemned as the expression of a materialistic and godless culture. The Catholic and Irish-language heritage of the remaining Irish-speaking areas constituted an important barrier against the corrupting influences of the anglophone world. Linguistically nonsense; sociolinguistically very revealing.

So, just as it had been reviled as the language of "popery," proscribed under the Tudors, used to facilitate religious conversion, and then indirectly proscribed again, the religious associations of the Irish language were exploited by nineteenth-century revivalists. The twists and turns of the Irish-English-Catholic-Protestant nexus are enough, in themselves, to justify greater sociolinguistic attention. That the strength of Catholicism, unwavering until the most recent times in Ireland, could be used to halt, shore up, and perhaps even reverse the decline of Irish seems a logical move. Indeed, if it had proved possible to convince the Catholic Irish that there was a necessary and indissoluble link between their faith and the Irish language, the fortunes of the latter might have shown a dramatic improvement.

In fact, religious strength may have acted *against* language-revival efforts. As the most broadly potent component of Irish identity, the continuity of Catholicism may have diluted the urge to protect the linguistic component. In the face of a powerful neighbor whose language increasingly seems the key to social and economic advance, a weakening local language may not seem so vital a pillar of "groupness" if another stalwart support remains secure. Even among activist minorities, a certain linguistic resignation may become increasingly apparent, a certain acceptance may grow, bolstered by the conviction that, after all, group identity is still on firm ground.

These Celtic linkages are not solely of the past. A contemporary Presbyterian minister in Scotland now suggests that, whatever may have once been the case, God is now quite clearly ill-disposed toward Gaelic. In the absence of Gaelic-speaking candidates for the ministry, the reverend gentleman has argued that "since the Lord is not sending out Gaelic-speaking labourers to toil in His harvest, I must draw the conclusion that it is not His will that Gaelic survive as a language."

There may be few Gaelic-speaking laborers at work today in the fields of the Lord, but in other parts of the world missionary activity has carried on almost unabated. Such religious activity has always been closely entwined with linguistic matters. There is not the slightest doubt that a great deal of extremely useful linguistic work has been accomplished by missionaries, not all of it undertaken merely in the service of expediting conversions. As Max Müller pointed out, missionaries often felt it part of their duty to "collect lists of words, and draw up grammars wherever they came in contact with a new race." Contemporary linguists have also pointed to the important role that missionaries have played and continue to play. There is an obvious tension, of course, because missionaries are engaged, however beneficent their motives may be, in cultural intervention. More pointedly, missionaries may have a real and scholarly interest in local cultures and languages, but they are generally opposed to local religions.

An obvious implication is that indigenous languages are learned, recorded, and used as evangelical tools. Victorian missionaries in Africa found it expedient to learn local languages, and so do the current members of the Summer Institute of Linguistics (SIL). Thousands of workers, in virtually every part of the world, have produced many important publications, including *Ethnologue*, a comprehensive catalogue of all the world's languages. It is updated regularly, and the latest (2013) edition is the sixteenth. Established in the 1930s and now based in Texas, SIL is in fact the more secular face of its partner, the Wycliffe Bible Translators. Scholars have described the organization as attempting to minimize its missionary role—in which its language activities are aimed at producing, distributing, and supporting vernacular versions of the Bible.

The religious use of language has a long history. In eighteenth- and nineteenth-century Ireland, for example, the vernacular was employed in hopes of more efficiently transforming Catholics into Protestants. A century earlier, Comenius, the great Czech educator, said, "let some of our own people, through intercourse with the barbarians learn their languages." He went further, suggesting that large numbers of children should be taken away to be educated and instructed in "our language and the harmonies of things," then returned as apostles to their own people. Again, a practice with a long and widespread history.

Many children in many parts of the world—including Australian and North American aboriginal children, whose removal and abuse are only now being subjected to systematic "truth-and-reconciliation" investigations—were routinely removed from their homes and placed in residential schools. The ostensible reason was always to better educate them in the ways of modernity and, therefore, to improve their prospects. More subtly, however, the aim was often to interrupt older traditions, cultures, and languages that were seen, at best, as passively primitive and, at worst, as actively opposed to the dictates of a conquering or a dominant power.

Evangelists have often found the need to teach as well as learn language. Early Jesuit missionaries, for instance, found that a diversity of tongues frustrated their activities: even where an indigenous lingua franca existed, "its primitive vocabulary was quite inadequate for explaining the *mysteria fidei.*" Thus, the early attempts at constructed languages, forerunners of Esperanto, were strongly religiously motivated. Spiritual impulses generally tallied well with less heavenly aims: merchant-adventurers in the Americas told Charles V that linguistic confusion interfered with the discovery and exploitation of gold, silver, and other valuable resources. So, in the preface to his seventeenth-century universal-language scheme, the *Ars Signorum*, George Dalgarno pointed out its value for "civilizing barbarous Nations, Propagating the Gospel, and encreasing Traffique and Commerce."

Language and gender

In obsolete usage, "gender" could refer to types or sorts: "diseases of this gender are for the most part incurable," wrote a seventeenth-century physician. As a verb, it once indicated copulation: "elephants never gender but in private, out of sight." By the mid-eighteenth century there had emerged the related sense of the getting of offspring: "from tigers tigers spring; pards gender pards." But, from at least the fourteenth century, "gender" was essentially a grammatical term. With one or two historical exceptions, often of a facetious or coy nature, the sense of the word as an indication of the masculine or feminine behavior of men and women is a modern usage. It is usually, and usefully, distinguished from "sex": biological characteristics define the latter, while gender, although built upon biological categorization, is a social construction.

There are of course actual language differences between genders, and some have been quite striking. When Europeans first came into contact with the Carib Indians of the New World, they found that both men and women had expressions "peculiar to themselves" (as a seventeenth-century report put it). Each

Box G
Gender in language

Words may refer to males or females, or to things that have become associated with these categories. In English, we find "he" and "she," "actor" and "actress," as well as some less obvious ascriptions (ships as feminine, for instance). Other languages also have a neuter gender (in English, "it" is a neuter pronoun). It can be difficult to understand some gender allocations. In German, for instance, "knife" (*messer*), "fork" (*gabel*), and "spoon" (*löffel*) are, respectively, neuter, feminine, and masculine. In French, *pénis* is masculine—but so is *vagin*. Italian sopranos are masculine, but the sentries are feminine. In both French and Italian the moon (*lune, luna*) is feminine, and the sun (*sole, soleil*) is masculine; in German, however, the moon (*mond*) is masculine, and the sun (*sonne*) is feminine. *Und so weiter*. And so on. *Et ainsi de suite. E così via.*

understood the other, but different activities and interests, accompanied and reinforced by social and religious taboos, had given rise to differences in actual usage. Perhaps—in principle if not in degree—things have not changed all that much over time and culture.

There are languages in which the sex of the *listener* rather than that of the speaker determines the variant used, and there are others in which the sex of *both* speaker and listener is influential. In many cultures, too, linguistic differences intertwine with conceptions and descriptions of kinship relationships. In the Chiquitano language of Bolivia, a woman says *ichibausi* to mean "my brother," where a man would say *tsaruki*; "my father" is *ishupu* for females, but *ijai* for males. One might argue, perhaps, that this sort of variation does not specifically or primarily implicate gender differences. After all, the relationship of a sister to her brother is not the same as that of brother to brother, and there is no reason why sisters and brothers should refer to other brothers with the same word. These are, then, different words for psychologically different things, rather than different words for the same things.

More familiar to most readers are less rigid language variations across genders: not so much "gender-exclusive" as "gender-preferential." It is a commonly reported generality that women's speech tends to be more "standard" and more "polite" than men's, that women are more conservative in their usage. A seemingly contradictory finding is that, where group language shift is under way, women tend to be early "shifters" to the more prestigious or dominant intruder. But the contradiction weakens with attention to just why women's speech should be more standard than men's. Many explanations link female linguistic conservatism with status-consciousness. If, for instance, women are less socially secure than men, they may wish to gain status through the use of more standard forms. If women have traditionally been less defined by markers of occupation and income, they may make their speech a

Name, sex, and religion

sort of surrogate status marker. If they are more concerned with their children's lives, they may wish to act as "better" linguistic role models. No doubt all of these possibilities have some explanatory value; none, of course, need be options of which speakers are consciously aware.

At the same time, women swear more often nowadays, at least in Western societies. Occupational and educational levels are relevant, but so is age: the four-letter words I regularly hear used by female undergraduates in the corridors are not nearly so frequent in the mouths of their women instructors, even when the latter are relaxing after work, even when they are in same-sex venues. Studies have also shown that, even in a more linguistically permissive age, there remain some words (fewer than before, no doubt) that women tend not to use. There is swearing and swearing.

If it is incorrect to simply say that men swear more than women do, caution should also be exercised when discussing politeness. Circumstances almost always alter cases, and the frequency, form, and function of polite usage is a matter for inquiry in either gender. Besides, although it is generally accepted as a desirable social lubricant that can make people feel safer and more comfortable, politeness that is seen as excessive or insincere is often associated with subordination, deference, even fawning. This, in turn, may reinforce its feminine connotations. Still, when we consider the regularity with which we hear empty requests ("Have a nice day!"), or have someone tell us who they are, for obviously venal reasons ("Hi! I'm Chuck, and I'll be your waiter this evening"), or are inappropriately reassured ("Hey! No problem"), and when all such noxious utterances blithely cross every conceivable social divide, it is possible to imagine that the currency has become so cheapened that it would be stupid to try and attach any gender nuances to its use.

If women's and men's speech reflects status differences, then matters of social convention—but also dominance and subordination—must be considered. If women are expected to use "better" forms than men, if they are supposed to be more "polite," if their use of profanity and obscenity is more severely sanctioned, then it might reasonably be concluded that they are a group whose linguistic (and other) behavior has limits placed upon it. It is ironic that the forms this limiting takes are often velvet-lined: isn't it good to be polite and to avoid swearing? The fact remains, however, that if women are on some sort of linguistic pedestal in these regards, they have been *placed* there, and pedestals offer little room for movement.

A subordinate social role can imply insecurity, uncertainty, and lack of confidence. It is exactly these features that were elucidated by Robin Lakoff in her studies of women's language in the 1970s. There were a number of difficulties with Lakoff's work, however. Her methodology was questionable, and her analysis was imprecise; her lists of features were hardly comprehensive; and she implicitly adopted a "male-as-norm" perspective. Nonetheless, her attempts to at least begin a classification of recurring gender differences in speech have been widely and favorably recognized.

Among the most interesting features are those involving either overstatement or understatement, because both can suggest nervousness, timidity, and a desire to mollify or to avoid unpleasantness. And these, in turn, are related to gender differences in communication. Men dominate conversations, men interrupt women more than women do men, and women provide more conversational feedback then men, making more encouraging and facilitating remarks during exchanges. This, at least, has been the received wisdom.

It would be easy to see all of this as evidence of clear-cut differences in which comparisons are not generally favorable to women. But what is easy is not always what is correct, and one or two points should be made. The speech characteristics traditionally associated with women are not exclusively theirs, the familiar features do not always signify the same thing, and a dominant-subordinate dichotomy is clearly an insufficiently nuanced perspective.

Consider "tag questions," one of the most widely discussed features of women's speech. Must they *always* imply uncertainty, do they *always* invite the listener to make a correction or at least expand upon a dubious utterance? Some clearly do ("It's a wonderful painting, isn't it?"), but others are better understood as "facilitative," giving the listener a comfortable conversational entry ("You've just changed jobs, haven't you?"), and others still may work to soften a criticism ("That was a bit silly, wasn't it?"). Readers will immediately see that these usages are frequently employed by both men and women. Tags can also be confrontational ("I just *told* you, didn't I?"), in which case readers would be right to believe that men are the more frequent users.

In a careful analysis, Janet Holmes found that most women's tag-question use (about 60 percent) was facilitative, a third expressed uncertainty, and only the small remainder had a mollifying function. Men's use was clearly less facilitative (about 25 percent), but about twice as likely to be used to "soften" or to express uncertainty. These findings seem to turn stereotypes on their heads. Can men's language really be so emollient? Can men really be more uncertain in their opinions than women? And if they are more apt to soften their views, why are they not more facilitative: wouldn't these tend to go together? Well, yes and no. Perhaps men are more linguistically aggressive than are women and hence feel a more frequent need to moderate their expressions. Perhaps they forge too quickly ahead with ill-informed points of view, only to have to back-pedal afterwards.

More fine-grained analyses of gender differences in speech reveal that "women's" features, greater female politeness, increased use of standard variants, and so on may all imply more about genuine facilitative and supportive desires than they do about insecurity and lack of confidence. Helena Leet-Pellegrini has succinctly remarked that men typically ask themselves if they have won in conversational exchanges, while women ponder whether or not they have been sufficiently helpful. This is a little too neat, but a broader point is that men and women may use language for different social purposes, having been socialized in different ways from earliest childhood. Even silence can differentiate: if a man is silent, this may be taken as a sign of care and wisdom, of authority and potency; if a woman is silent, she may be viewed as weak or uncertain. Here is another irony, inasmuch as women in many cultures have had silence imposed upon them in one way or another.

Alleged differences in men's and women's gossip are instructive. The latter is traditionally seen to focus on personal relationships, experiences, and problems, in a generally supportive atmosphere in which "networking" is key. The former is supposedly more concerned with factual information, often in a competitive or combative format (of course, the tradition for men avoids the word "gossip" altogether.) And yet, who could deny the centrality of factual exchange to much of women's networking? Who imagines that men are unwilling or incapable of spending time in idle banter?

There is a large popular literature on miscommunication between men and women, and while some books build upon all-too-real social conventions and stereotypes, there is also a great deal of exaggeration for humorous effect. When ways of curbing miscommunication are discussed, Deborah Cameron suggests, the books turn into self-help guides aimed at women, part of the much larger genre that could be styled "you and your relationship" or, indeed, "how to deal with your man." Other "advice" has told women to speak more like men if they want to be taken seriously, to do well in the corporate world, and so on. At best, then, these are recommendations for adaptation and tolerance rather than reasons for either behavior or stereotypes. Cameron also points out that gender variations are underpinned by power variations: when a husband asks his wife if there is any ketchup, the real message is "(please) bring me some"; if a daughter asks her mother the same thing, she is more likely to be told that the bottle is in the cupboard.

Besides sex or gender differences in language use, there is also the matter of sexist language itself. Leaving aside truly violent or repulsive usage—which, especially if one were to consider image as well as language, is actually increasing, thanks to the ever-more ubiquitous visual media—our culture continues to provide frequent instances of crude, trivializing, stereotyped, or offensive language.

Only a generation ago, it was still possible to find these sorts of examples: "Barrister and woman found dead" (newspaper headline); "Drivers: belt the wife and kids—and keep them safe" (road-safety poster); "If it were a lady, it would get its bottom pinched" (Fiat advertisement). Today, we are a little more careful (not in all quarters, of course), but a caring public face does not necessarily imply an altered private one. Besides, things like "delegates and their wives" sometimes still slip under the radar, despite current attention, omnipresent writers' guidelines, and so on. The linguistics scholar Suzanne Romaine writes of being referred to as the only "lady professor" at Merton College. Not in all quarters, indeed. Given all this, should we try and change society, secure in the knowledge that language change will follow? Should we make attempts at language reform, as a way of speeding the happy day? Is language only a symptom, or could it also be a contributor? Efforts continue and obviously should do so along both fronts. At the level of language change, it is clear that some egregious usages have disappeared, and some new and more appropriate terms have arisen. "Ms." found a permanent place quite quickly, after all.

Otto Jespersen, the great Danish linguist and anglicist, stood at the head of a long line of later authors, both male and female, when he included in his *Language* (1922) a chapter on women—but none on men. The gender-and-language literature used to deal almost exclusively with women, and much of it still does. There are sociological reasons for this. Just as it can be more instructive to study Spanish rather than English language policies in the United States, just as it may be more appropriate to consider the social situation of blacks rather than whites, so a stronger focus on women's language may be more revealing. Still, despite recent advances in both information and social sensitivity, we must take care to avoid treating the speech of one gender as the norm from which that of the other differs or deviates. Why say women are more polite than men, or swear less, or are more conversationally facilitative, or hedge their linguistic bets? Why not ask, rather, why men are ruder, more confrontational, and more unreasonably assertive? An analysis of tag questions that built upon Janet Holmes's insights had as its title "Not gender difference, but the difference gender makes," and this apt phrase is relevant to all investigations in the area.

Naming ourselves

The study of names (onomastics) is a minor interest within sociolinguistics, even though everyone realizes that names are significant. Contemporary research reveals that people whose names are rare or strange can do less well at school; they are called upon less frequently by teachers, and they may receive lower marks. Studies have also shown that different names attached to the same academic work or employment résumé can elicit different assessments. Most parents spend a lot of time thinking about names for their children, and they are right to do so.

The names Faith, Felicity, Patience, and Joy are modern reminders of Puritan practices, in which godly virtues were made into names. Increase Mather was an important figure in seventeenth-century Massachusetts, and Praisegod Barebone gave his name to a parliamentary assembly of 1653. Readers of Patrick O'Brian's sea stories will think of Jack Aubrey's steward, the loyal but surly Preserved Killick. More elaborate naming also occurred along the same lines: some rejoiced in names like Fight-the-Good-Fight Jones and Fear-the-Lord Smith.

Contemporary first names like Courage, Goodwill, Blessed, Lordwin, Goodluck, and Withus remain popular in parts of Africa, legacies of colonialism and proselytism. Even without overtly religious intent, the imposition of foreign names remains a colonial reminder. Rolihlahla Mandela recounts how, on his first day at school, the teacher (Miss Mdingane) told him that his new name would be Nelson. It is not surprising, then, to find that indigenous names are often taken up again in postcolonial settings. In South Africa, the premier of the Eastern Cape went from Arnold to Makhenkesi; the defense minister, from Patrick to Mosioua.

Group names are no less informative. Variants along the lines of "the people of the river" or "the mountain-dwellers" are common, but so are names that simply signify "us" in some way. One may imagine this mild enough, but in many instances the "us" really means "the real people," "the first people" or, indeed, "the human beings." This obviously tells us something about views held of others. Such names are found in many parts of the world—in Japan (the Ainu), in Africa (Bantu and Berber), in North America (Inuit, Cherokee, Salish), and elsewhere. The Asmat of Irian Jaya provide an extreme example; while they are "the human beings," they classify everyone else as *manowe*: the "edible ones."

"Outsiders" are regularly given names that are not of their own choosing, and sometimes these external ascriptions come to dominate. Some of the Dakota ("the friends") became known as Sioux ("snakes"), an abbreviation of a term bestowed upon them by enemies. Many Inuit consider the earlier term "Eskimo" to be a derogatory reference to them as eaters of raw meat. While the

Welsh call themselves *Cymry* (meaning something like "fellow countrymen"), the English name for them derives from the Anglo-Saxon *w(e)alh*, via the Germanic *Wälsche* ("stranger," "foreigner," or even "barbarian"). The Khoisan speakers of southern Africa call themselves *Khoekhoe* ("men of men"), but the Dutch called them Hottentots ("stammerers"). Barbarians and stammerers: the terms are in fact closely associated. The first, signifying all that is brutal, uncouth, and tasteless, is derived from a Greek term for the latter.

The rancor caused by external naming is unsurprising. It can be understood as a specific manifestation of the bitterness arising from "voice appropriation," the practice in which important group myths and legends are largely told by outsiders. This is seen as cultural theft and a continuation of colonialism. Since, in many cultures, the narrative care of sacred or semisacred names, stories, and legends is assigned to certain families or individuals, the injury is exacerbated. Think of the shamans of North America, or the European bards, or the griots of West Africa: they are living libraries, charged with the preservation and transmission of the most central and important group narratives.

But "appropriation" must be put in quotation marks because, no matter how much one may sympathize with individuals and cultures who have been badly treated, the matter is by no means clear-cut. A logical extension of the appropriation argument might lead to the conclusion that no one could ever write about anything beyond one's own immediate experience; only "insiders" could write about their lives and cultures. It would follow, then, that women are never to write about men, blacks never about whites, Germans never about Spaniards. This is a nonsensical imposition that would have stifled a huge proportion of the world's literature and of the knowledge that human beings have of one another. Still, it is easy to understand the grievances that arise when the narrative boundaries that are breached separate groups of significantly different socioeconomic clout. Sauce for the goose may, logically, be sauce for the gander, but real-life inequalities surely suggest some special attention to the less powerful. The more thoughtful commentaries on "voice appropriation" have therefore not stated matters in some either-or fashion but instead have argued about the *degree* of cross-border commentary that might be reasonable, and the circumstances and contexts in which it ought or ought not to occur.

A final note

Name, religion, and gender are three of the most important features of individual and group distinctiveness—and when they are linked with language, even more potent identity marking emerges. The preceding chapters have essentially led to the specifics of this final one, through a consideration of the questions of identity that underpin virtually all aspects of sociolinguistics and the sociology of language. While language is a dynamic entity whose course can be mapped across centuries and cultures, across classes and contexts, it always retains its powerful function as a reflection and a shaper of "groupness" in one form or another. It follows that attitudes toward languages and language varieties— attitudes that reflect perceptions of their speakers—are central components of the "social life of language."

Efforts to "protect" language and keep it free from unwanted contamination are entirely predictable, particularly when the distinction between language as instrument and language as symbol has been understood. Language may be defended on purely instrumental grounds—to maintain clarity and to prevent ambiguity, for example. Deeper prescriptive impulses arise, however, when the integrity and the strength of the linguistic markers of group boundaries are seen to be threatened. Risks here can come from within a language (nonstandard dialects of low social status, for example) or from the external pressures created by large linguistic neighbors. These tensions can fuel attempts to maintain or rejuvenate endangered varieties, but they may also lead to patterns of language shift and loss. Bilingual or bidialectal accommodations may also be sought.

In sum, language is an ever-changing feature of human life and is one of the most revealing windows through which to contemplate our social definitions and interactions.

References

General

Some of the material in this book draws upon information published in my earlier work, several specific references to which are found in the following notes.

Excellent recent overviews of sociolinguistics can be found in Raj Mesthrie, ed., *The Cambridge Handbook of Sociolinguistics* (Cambridge: Cambridge University Press, 2011); Raj Mesthrie, Joan Swann, Andrea Deumert, and William Leap, eds., *Introducing Sociolinguistics* (Edinburgh: Edinburgh University Press, 2009); Martin Ball, ed., *The Routledge Handbook of Sociolinguistics Around the World* (Oxford: Routledge, 2010); Ruth Wodak, Barbara Johnstone, and Paul Kerswill, eds., *The Sage Handbook of Sociolinguistics* (Thousand Oaks, CA: Sage, 2011); and Nikolas Coupland and Adam Jaworski, eds., *Sociolinguistics*, 6 vols. (Oxford: Routledge, 2008). "Globalization" has become a bad word in many quarters, but see Jan Blommaert's balanced treatment in *Sociolinguistics of Globalization* (Cambridge: Cambridge University Press, 2010).

There is also good recent coverage of specific areas, some of it extensive. See Brian Joseph and Hope Dawson, eds., *Historical Linguistics*, 4 vols. (Oxford: Routledge, 2012); Peter Austin and Stuart McGill, eds., *Endangered Languages*, 4 vols. (Oxford: Routledge, 2012); Nancy Hornberger, ed., *Educational Linguistics*, 6 vols. (Oxford: Routledge, 2011). The scope of the last collection is considerably wider than its title implies. James Simpson's single-volume collection, *Handbook of Applied Linguistics* (Oxford: Routledge, 2011), is also useful. These and other titles remind readers that sociolinguistic matters are often discussed under other, related headings. For example, in a citation in Simpson's book, Chris Brumfit observes that applied linguistics deals with "investigation of real-world problems in which language is a central issue" (p. 2). While applied linguistics is often seen as a component in decision or policy making, this thrust obviously overlaps with matters also treated under the rubric of sociolinguistics: a clear demonstration of this can be found in Christopher Hall, Patrick Smith, and Rachel Wicaksono, eds., *Mapping Applied Linguistics* (Oxford: Routledge, 2011); and Li Wei and Vivian Cook, eds., *Contemporary Applied Linguistics*, 2 vols. (London: Continuum, 2009).

Chapter 1: Coming to terms

Suketoshi Tanabe published *Gengo-shakaigaku* in 1936 (Tokyo: Nikko Shoin); the title may be given as *Sociolinguistics* or *Sociology of Language*. See also Thomas Hodson, "Sociolinguistics in India," *Man in India* 19 (1939); and Haver Currie, "A Projection of Socio-linguistics: The Relationship of Speech to Social Status," *Southern Speech Journal* 18 (1952): 28–37.

For languages as "separable and enumerable" categories, see Sinfree Makoni and Alastair Pennycook, *Disinventing and Reconstituting Languages* (Bristol: Multilingual Matters, 2007), 2. For "colorless green ideas sleep furiously," see Noam Chomsky, *Syntactic Structures* (The Hague: Mouton, 1957), 15. Max Weinreich reported (but did not coin) the phrase, "a language is a dialect that has an army and navy" in "Der YIVO un di problemen fun undzer tsayt," *YIVO-Bleter* 25 (1945): 3–18. Maurice Olender referred to the "academic identity card" provided by Sir William "Oriental" Jones, in "Europe, or How to Escape Babel," *History and Theory* 33 (1994): 5–25, quote on 8. The extract in box A is taken from the "discourse" delivered by William Jones to the Asiatick Society of Bengal in 1786.

Chapter 2: Variation and change

Principles of Linguistic Change is William Labov's three-volume work (Oxford: Wiley-Blackwell, 1994–2010). See also Robert Bayley and Ceil Lucas, eds., *Sociolinguistic Variation* (Cambridge: Cambridge University Press, 2007); Jack Chambers, *Sociolinguistic*

Theory: Linguistic Variation and Its Social Significance (Oxford: Wiley-Blackwell, 2009); and Peter Trudgill, *Sociolinguistic Variation and Change* (Georgetown: Georgetown University Press, 2002). More focused works include Warren Maguire and April McMahon, eds., *Analysing Variation in English* (Cambridge: Cambridge University Press, 2011); and Nancy Dorian, *Investigating Variation* (Oxford: Oxford University Press, 2010). *Language Variation and Change* is a Cambridge journal, published since 1989.

The Dickens extracts are from *David Copperfield*, chaps. 39 and 61. For "does 'news' sound like . . ." see Stefan Dollinger, "The Written Questionnaire as a Sociolinguistic Data Gathering Tool: Testing its Validity," *Journal of English Linguistics* 40 (2012): 74–110, quote on 74. Dollinger also discusses Wenker's nineteenth-century work in Germany.

For Labov's work in Massachusetts and New York, see his *Sociolinguistic Patterns* (Philadelphia: University of Pennsylvania Press, 1972). The direct citations are from his article, "Some Principles of Linguistic Methodology," *Language in Society* 1 (1972): 97–120, quotes on 109 and 113. For the follow-up work mentioned here, see Renée Blake and Meredith Josey, "The /ay/ Diphthong in a Martha's Vineyard Community," *Language in Society* 32 (2003): 451–85; and John Tierney, "Can We Talk?" *New York Times Magazine*, January 1995, 16. Labov's other famous study is reexamined in Patrick-André Mather, "The Social Stratification of /r/ in New York City: Labov's Department Store Study Revisited," *Journal of English Linguistics* 40 (2012): 338–56.

The material in box B is taken from Peter Trudgill, *Accent, Dialect and the School* (London: Edward Arnold, 1975). For *hambag*, see Jean Aitchison, *Language Change* (London: Fontana, 1981), 135. For *in'* and *ing* endings, see ibid., 80; Mark Liberman's "Language Log" (www.languagelog.ldc. upenn.edu) for May 10, 2004; and John Fischer, "Social Influences on the Choice of a Linguistic Variant" *Word* 14 (1958): 47–56. For the work reviewed by Lynda Mugglestone, see her *Talking Proper* (Oxford: Oxford University Press, 1995); the direct quotations are found on 106, 108, and 127; see also Raymond Chapman, *Forms of Speech in Victorian Fiction* (London: Longman, 1994).

For hypercorrection, see William Labov, *Sociolinguistic Patterns* (Philadelphia: University of Pennsylvania Press, 1972); Charles Boberg,

"The Attitudinal Component of Variation in American English Foreign <a> Nativization," *Journal of Language and Social Psychology* 18 (1999): 49–61; and Katherine Jones, *Accent on Privilege* (Philadelphia: Temple University Press, 2001). On covert prestige, see Peter Trudgill, *Sociolinguistics* (London: Penguin, 2000). For three books with the word "Bullshit" in their titles, see Harry Frankfurt, *On Bullshit* (Princeton, NJ: Princeton University Press, 2005); Nick Webb, *The Dictionary of Bullshit* (London: Robson Books, 2005); and Laura Penny, *Your Call Is Important to Us: The Truth about Bullshit* (Toronto: McClelland & Stewart, 2005).

For George Orwell on effeminacy, see his *Inside the Whale and Other Essays* (London: Penguin, 1964), 74. On switching behavior, see Shana Poplack, "Sometimes I'll Start a Sentence in English *y terminó en español*," *Linguistics* 18 (1980): 581–618. For Jack Chambers's observation, see his *Sociolinguistic Theory* (Oxford: Wiley-Blackwell, 2009), 206.

Chapter 3: Perceptions of language

For the best recent overview, see Peter Garrett, *Attitudes to Language* (Cambridge: Cambridge University Press 2010). See also Howard Giles and John Edwards, "Attitudes to Language: Past, Present and Future," in *The Routledge Linguistics Encyclopaedia*, ed. Kirsten Malmkjær (Oxford: Routledge, 2010). For the most recent brief overview of "amateur" views of language, see Antje Wilson and Martin Stegu, eds., *Applied Folk Linguistics* (Amsterdam: Benjamins, 2011). The "matched-guise" technique made its first appearance in Wallace Lambert, Robert Hodgson, Robert Gardner, and Steven Fillenbaum, eds., "Evaluational Reactions to Spoken Languages," *Journal of Abnormal and Social Psychology* 60 (1960): 44–51. A great deal of subsequent work was done by Howard Giles and his colleagues: for an overview, see Howard Giles and Mikaela Marlow, "Theorizing Language Attitudes," in *Communication Yearbook* 35, ed. Charles Salmon (Oxford: Routledge, 2011).

My Dublin study is "Students' Reactions to Irish Regional Accents," *Language and Speech* 20 (1977): 280–86. On African American vernacular English, see William Labov, *Language in the Inner City* (Philadelphia: University of Pennsylvania Press, 1976).

For RP as the "most pleasing and sonorous form" of English, see Henry Wyld, *The Best English* (Oxford: Clarendon, 1934), 3. As the "most subtle and most beautiful": see Robert Chapman "Oxford English," *Society for Pure English* 4, no. 37 (1932): 562. The Canadian journalist referred to is Russell Smith; see his "Who Knew 'nooz' Was About Morality?" *Globe & Mail* (Toronto), 20 December 2007. On the "imposed norm" and "inherent value" studies, the "minority-group reaction," and the persistence of low-status varieties, see the work of Howard Giles, Wallace Lambert, Ellen Ryan, and their colleagues, in John Edwards, *Language and Identity* (Cambridge: Cambridge University Press, 2009). Michael Halliday's comment is from his "The Users and Uses of Language," in *Readings in the Sociology of Language*, ed. Joshua Fishman (The Hague: Mouton, 1968), 165. For the anecdote reported in box C, I am indebted to Robert Zecker.

The discussion of discourse analysis is drawn largely from chap. 2 in Edwards, *Language Diversity in the Classroom* (Bristol: Multilingual Matters, 2010). See also Jan Blommaert's *Discourse* (Cambridge: Cambridge University Press, 2005); James Gee and Michael Handford, eds., *Routledge Handbook of Discourse Analysis* (Oxford: Routledge, 2011); and Christina Paulston, Scott Kiesling, and Elizabeth Rangel, eds., *The Handbook of Intercultural Discourse and Communication* (New York: Wiley-Blackwell, 2012).

For "language and the social world are mutually shaping . . ." and "situated language use," see Ben Rampton, Karin Tusting, Janet Maybin, Richard Barwell, Angela Creese, and Vally Lytra, "U.K. Linguistic Ethnography" (www.ling-ethnog.org.uk/documents/papers/ramptonetal2004.pdf; accessed September 2012), 2. On the classroom contributions of boys and girls, see Allyson Julé, *Gender, Participation, and Silence in the Classroom* (London: Palgrave-Macmillan, 2004). For "an extraordinarily high ratio . . ." see James Coleman, "Review of *Studies in Ethnomethodology*," *American Sociological Review* 33 (1968): 126–30, quote on 130. For "political discourse, media . . . ," "upfront about its own . . ." and "representativeness, selectivity . . ." see Jan Blommaert, *Discourse* (Cambridge: Cambridge University Press, 2005), 6, 21, and 31. For "discourse analysis with attitude," see Teun van Dijk, "Multidisciplinary CDA: A Plea for Diversity," in *Methods of Critical Discourse Analysis*, ed. Ruth Wodak and Michael Meyer (Thousand Oaks, CA: Sage, 2001), 96. Henry Widdowson's observation is in his *Text, Context, Pretext: Critical Issues in Discourse Analysis* (Oxford: Wiley-Blackwell, 2004), 173.

The 600-page study is Alan Grimshaw's *Collegial Discourse* (Norwood, NJ: Ablex, 1989); his later comments are from his edited collection, *What's Going on Here?* (Norwood, NJ: Ablex, 1994); see especially 453. For the famous 1:1 map, see Jorge Luis Borges, *Collected Fictions* (London: Penguin, 1999). And, for "students of spoken interaction," see the last page of Alan Firth's review of Grimshaw's two books, *American Journal of Sociology* 101 (1996): 1487–92.

Chapter 4: Protecting language

For a discussion of Claude Favre de Vaugelas, and for the observation about Cardinal Richelieu, see Robert Hall, *External History of the Romance Languages* (New York: Elsevier, 1974), 180. On the dialects of Gascony, etc., see Douglas Kibbee, "Patriotic Roots of Prescriptivism" (paper presented at the "Prescriptivism and Patriotism" conference, Toronto, 2009). Randolph Quirk wrote about "amateur do-gooders" and Webster's "odious distinctions" in his *Style and Communication in the English Language* (London: Edward Arnold, 1982), 65 and 99. For the "force of common usage," see Glendon Drake, *The Role of Prescriptivism in American Linguistics, 1820–1870* (Amsterdam: Benjamins, 1977), 9. See Lynda Mugglestone, "Patriotism, Empire and Cultural Prescriptivism" (paper presented at the "Prescriptivism and Patriotism" conference, Toronto, 2009) for "a good language . . ." and "patriotic endeavour."

The single most comprehensive overview of language planning is that of Robert Kaplan and Richard Baldauf, *Language Planning: From Practice to Theory* (Bristol: Multilingual Matters, 1997); Kaplan and Baldauf are also the editors of the Routledge journal, *Current Issues in Language Planning* (established 2000). A more venerable journal is *Language Problems and Language Planning*, established in 1977 and edited by Humphrey Tonkin for Benjamins. The citation of Elie Kedourie can be found on page 125 of his *Nationalism* (Westport, CT: Praeger, 1961).

The quotation about "functioning ecologies" is in Peter Mühlhäusler's "Language Planning and Language Ecology," *Current Issues in Language Planning* 1 (2000): 306–67, quote on 308. For "ancestral cultures . . ." and "only one language . . . ," see Salikoko Mufwene, "Colonisation, Globalisation and the Future of Languages in the Twenty-first Century," *International Journal on Multicultural Societies* 4 (2002): 162–93, quotes on 176 and 177–78. For "without romanticizing . . .," see Tapani Salminen, "Minority Languages in a Society in Turmoil," in *Endangered Languages*, ed. Nicholas Ostler (Bath: Foundation for Endangered Languages, 1998), 62. The fulsome book dedication is by Luisa Maffi, in her collection, *On Biocultural Diversity* (Washington, DC: Smithsonian Institution, 2001). Frank Polzenhagen and René Dirven provide the comment about "pronounced anti-globalisation . . ." in "Rationalist or Romantic Model in Language Policy and Globalisation" (paper presented at the "Linguistic Agency" conference, Landau, 2004). Peter Mühlhäusler asks scholars to be "shop stewards for linguistic diversity" in his *Linguistic Ecology* (Oxford: Routledge, 1996), 2.

Chapter 5: Languages great and small

The translator of Lucretius is Ronald Latham; the citation is in *On the Nature of the Universe* (London: Penguin, 1973), 15. For Voltaire's remark about German, see John Waterman, *A History of the German Language* (Seattle: University of Washington Press, 1966), 138. For the various sentiments cited in the paragraph beginning "In the early seventeenth century . . . ," see Tony Crowley's *Standard English and the Politics of Language* (London: Palgrave-Macmillan, 2003); see also Ronald Wardhaugh, *Languages in Competition* (Oxford: Blackwell, 1987); Lynda Mugglestone's *Talking Proper* (Oxford: Oxford University Press, 1995); and Raymond Chapman, *Forms of Speech in Victorian Fiction* (London: Longman, 1994).

For Robert of Gloucester's observation, see Charles Barber, *The English Language* (Cambridge: Cambridge University Press, 1993), 136. Fuller details of John Florio (box D) can be found in Frances Yates, *John Florio* (Cambridge: Cambridge University Press, 1934).

See Sue Wright, *Language Policy and Language Planning* (London: Palgrave-Macmillan, 2004), 168, for "the acceptance of English . . ."; see also David Crystal, *English as a Global Language* (Cambridge: Cambridge University Press, 2003) and *Language and the Internet* (Cambridge: Cambridge University Press, 2006); and Joshua Fishman, Andrew Conrad, and Alma Rubal-Lopez, eds., *Post-imperial English* (The Hague: Mouton de Gruyter, 1996).

For the stance taken by Ngũgĩ wa Thiong'o, see his "On Writing in Gikuyu," *Research in African Literatures* 16 (1985): 151–55 and

Decolonising the Mind (London: Currey, 1986); see also Chinua Achebe, *Morning Yet on Creation Day* (New York: Doubleday, 1975).

Chapter 6: Loyalty, maintenance, shift, loss, and revival

For Fredrik Barth's views on cultural continuity, see his edited collection, *Ethnic Groups and Boundaries* (Boston: Little, Brown, 1969). For "the lack of will to stop shrinking . . ." see Desmond Fennell, "Can a Shrinking Linguistic Minority Be Saved?" in *Minority Languages Today*, ed. Einar Haugen, J. Derrick McClure and Derick Thomson (Edinburgh: Edinburgh University Press, 1981), 38.

On "penury, drudgery and backwardness," see Caoimhín Ó Danachair, "The Gaeltacht," in *A View of the Irish Language*, ed. Brian Ó Cuív (Dublin: Government Stationery Office, 1969), 120. For "toil, hardship and scarcity" and "refinement and culture," see Charles Dunn, *High-land Settler: A Portrait of the Scottish Gael in Nova Scotia* (Toronto: University of Toronto Press, 1953), 134. John Lorne Campbell's "Scottish Gaelic in Canada," *American Speech* 11 (1936): 128–36, quote on 130, is the source of "carried with them the idea that. . . ." The citations from Ernest Renan are from his famous 1882 discourse, "Qu'est-ce qu'une nation?"; see Henriette Psichari, ed., *Oeuvres complètes de Ernest Renan* (Paris: Calmann-Lévy, 1947), 899 and 903.

The quotation from Joshua Fishman is in his "Whorfianism of the Third Kind," *Language in Society* 11 (1982): 1–14, quote on 8; see also his *Reversing Language Shift* (Bristol: Multilingual Matters, 1991).

Chapter 7: Multilingualism

Nikolas Coupland's *Style* (Cambridge: Cambridge University Press, 2007) and Susan Gass and Alison Mackey, eds., *The Routledge Handbook of Second Language Acquisition* (Oxford: Routledge, 2011) are recommended.

For Whorfianism and the Inuit, see Geoffrey Pullum, *The Great Eskimo Vocabulary Hoax* (Chicago: University of Chicago Press, 1991); and Edwards, *Language and Identity* (Cambridge: Cambridge University Press, 2009). Sherlock Holmes made his observation to Watson in *A Study in Scarlet* (London: Ward Lock, 1887). James Murray's letter may be found in his granddaughter's biography,

Caught in the Web of Words (New Haven, CT: Yale University Press, 1977), 70.

On "the use of a foreign language in the home . . ." see Florence Goodenough's "Racial Differences in the Intelligence of School Children," *Journal of Experimental Psychology* 9 (1926): 388–97, quote on 393. For the later bilingualism studies mentioned here, see Edwards, *Multilingualism* (London: Penguin, 1995), and "Bilingualism and Multilingualism," in *Handbook of Bilingualism and Multilingualism*, ed. Tej Bhatia and William Ritchie (New York: Wiley-Blackwell, 2013). The citations about "mental flexibility" and the "correlational problem" are in Robert Gardner and Wallace Lambert's *Attitudes and Motivation in Second-Language Learning* (Rowley, MA: Newbury House, 1972), 277.

Orwell's observation about "sheer dirtiness of fighting . . ." first appeared in his "As I Please" column, *Tribune* (UK), 28 January 1944. On the readily available data for Esperanto, see James Lieberman, "Esperanto and Trans-national Identity," *International Journal of the Sociology of Language* 20 (1979): 89–107, quote on 100. For the references to Dryden, Rieu, and Škvorecký, see my *Multilingualism* (London: Penguin). George Steiner's note about "hoarded dreams" is found in his *After Babel* (Oxford: Clarendon, 1992), 244.

Chapter 8: Name, sex, and religion

Good recent studies of language and religion include Tope Omoniyi's two edited works, *The Sociology of Language and Religion* (London: Palgrave Macmillan, 2010) and (with Joshua Fishman) *Explorations in the Sociology of Language and Religion* (Amsterdam: Benjamins, 2006). For further details regarding the section on religion, see Edwards, *Language and Identity* (Cambridge: Cambridge University Press, 2009). The Thomas Hobbes citations are from *Leviathan* (London: Crooke, 1651); see pages 12–13 in the Dent edition (1973); Max Müller's quotes are in his *Lectures on the Science of Language* (London: Longman, 1862), 129 and 135. See also Umberto Eco's *Search for the Perfect Language* (Oxford: Blackwell, 1995).

Fullerton's observation is in his *Prudence of St. Patrick's Irish Policy* (Dublin: O'Brien & Ards, 1916), 6. For the absence of Gaelic-speaking laborers, see Donald Meek, "God and Gaelic," in *Aithne na nGael—Gaelic*

Identities, ed. Gordon McCoy and Maolcholaim Scott (Belfast: Queen's University Institute of Irish Studies), 44.

Fuller discussion of the Summer Institute of Linguistics, of the material in box G, and of the now politically incorrect gender usages will be found in Edwards, *Language and Identity*. Comenius's observations are from his *Via Lucis Vestigata et Vestiganda*, first published in 1668; see Ernest Campagnac's translation (Liverpool: Liverpool University Press, 1938), 226–27. On the *mysteria fidei*, see Dilwyn Knox, "Ideas on Gesture and Universal Languages, ca. 1550–1650," in *New Perspectives on Renaissance Thought*, ed. John Henry and Sarah Hutton (London: Duckworth, 1990), 127.

On the Carib and South American Indians, see Peter Trudgill's *Sociolinguistics* (London: Penguin, 2000); the direct quotation referring to the seventeenth-century report is on 65. Robin Lakoff's work first found book form in *Language and Woman's Place* (New York: Harper & Row, 1975). See also Janet Holmes, *Introduction to Sociolinguistics* (London: Longman, 1992); Sara Mills, *Gender and Politeness* (Cambridge: Cambridge University Press, 2006); Deborah Cameron and Don Kulick, *Language and Sexuality* (Cambridge: Cambridge University Press, 2003); and Deborah Cameron, *Verbal Hygiene* (Oxford: Routledge, 1995). Helena Leet-Pellegrini's remark is in her "Conversational Dominance as a Function of Gender and Expertise," in *Language: Social Psychological Perspectives*, ed. Howard Giles, Peter Robinson, and Philip Smith (Oxford: Pergamon, 1980). Suzanne Romaine is the Merton "lady professor" noted in *Communicating Gender* (Hillsdale, NJ: Erlbaum, 1999); "Not Gender Difference but the Difference Gender Makes" is the title of an article by Deborah Cameron, *International Journal of the Sociology of Language* 94 (1992): 13–26.

For names in Africa, see Busi Makoni et al., "Naming Practices and Language Planning in Zimbabwe," *Current Issues in Language Planning* 8 (2007): 437–67; see also Nelson Mandela, *Long Walk to Freedom* (Boston: Little, Brown, 1994). George Stewart's *Names on the Globe* (Oxford: Oxford University Press, 1975) provided much useful information about group names.

Index

V

Vaugelas, Claude Favre de, 48
Velázquez, Isidro, 73
verbal hygiene, 53
Virgil, 95
"voice appropriation," 115–16
Voltaire (François-Marie Arouet), 61

W

Webster, Noah, 51–52
Weinreich, Max, 9

Wells, John, 27
Wenker, Georg, 20
Whorf, Benjamin Lee, 82
Whorfianism, 82–83
Wilson, Thomas (Bishop), 52
Winchester, Simon, 49
Wittgenstein, Ludwig, 7
Wycliffe Bible Translators, 104

Z

Zamenhof, Ludwig, 91
Zola, Émile, 96

SOCIAL MEDIA
Very Short Introduction

Join our community
www.oup.com/vsi

- Join us online at the official Very Short Introductions **Facebook** page.
- Access the thoughts and musings of our authors with our online **blog**.
- Sign up for our monthly **e-newsletter** to receive information on all new titles publishing that month.
- Browse the full range of Very Short Introductions online.
- Read **extracts** from the Introductions for free.
- Visit our library of **Reading Guides**. These guides, written by our expert authors will help you to question again, why you think what you think.
- If you are a teacher or lecturer you can order inspection copies quickly and simply via our website.

ONLINE CATALOGUE
A Very Short Introduction

Our online catalogue is designed to make it easy to find your ideal Very Short Introduction. View the entire collection by subject area, watch author videos, read sample chapters, and download reading guides.

http://fds.oup.com/www.oup.co.uk/general/vsi/index.html